UNIVERSITY OF WOLVERHAMPTON

Dudley Learning Centre

Castle View
Dudley DY1 3HR

Wolverhampton (01902) 323559

Telephone Renewals: 01902 321333
This item may be recalled at any time. Keeping it after it has
been recalled or beyond the date stamped may result in a fine.
See tariff of fines displayed at the counter.

/1 MAY 2003		
	13 NOV 2007	
1 1 JUN 2004		
– 8 APR 2005		
– 3 MAY 2005		
– 7 OCT 2005		

Th   War

FI   TON

UNIVERSITY OF WOLVERHAMPTON
LIBRARY

Acc No. **2160402**	CLASS	
CONTROL 0003270092	327.	
DATE –8 MAR 1999	SITE Dy	090U MAC

KT-443-153

WITHDRAWN

Collins
Educational
An Imprint of
HarperCollins*Publishers*

WP 2160402 9

Contents

About this book

This book is about the history of the Cold War. The content is arranged into five units.

On the first page of each unit the book makes clear exactly what you are going to find out about and what key questions the unit will answer.

Then come two or more pages called 'setting the scene'. These give you some of the basic information you will need in order to work through the rest of the unit. You will find these pages useful later if you have to revise this topic for the GCSE examinations.

The rest of each unit is called 'issues and enquiries'. These tell you a lot more about the history, topic by topic, but they all have plenty for you to do: investigations to follow up, simulation games and discussions. They also include assessment questions. These are aimed at the assessment objectives for GCSE. You should be able to:

– remember what you have learnt, recall it to mind and then select and organise this information in answer to a question;
– describe what happened in the historical periods and topics you have studied;
– explain why the things you have described were like that and how they happened that way;
– understand how other people explain and interpret the past;
– analyse and use different kinds of historical evidence to find out about the past.

There are plenty of other interesting things in the book – but you'll find out about those when you get to them!

The Cold War
1945 to 1989

The Cold War was a time (from 1945 to 1989) when the two greatest nations on Earth – the large, rich and powerful USA and USSR – lived in a state of constant hostility and fear, without actually fighting face to face. A struggle against a common enemy during the Second World War broke down almost as soon as the war ended and was replaced by a climate of distrust. Soviet and American leaders held opposing ideological views and had rival political ambitions. Their peoples were suspicious and scornful of each other. Their governments produced a steady stream of propaganda. Their factories produced millions of tonnes of deadly weapons, including vast stockpiles of nuclear missiles.

For over 40 years, these Cold War tensions affected the whole world. Quarrels between the two 'superpowers' (as the USA and USSR became known) led to wars in many lands, and few nations remained uninvolved. At times, people even feared that the Cold War might 'hot up' and lead to full-scale nuclear conflict. Then all life on our planet might have come to an end.

Fortunately, worldwide nuclear war did not happen. And, as you will discover as you read this book, the two superpowers finally found a way of making peace. Although the Cold War is now over, it still influences many people's lives. The superpowers and their former client states have had to come to terms with the big changes and adapt to new roles.

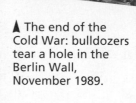

▲ The end of the Cold War: bulldozers tear a hole in the Berlin Wall, November 1989.

◄ Military power: Soviet nuclear missiles on show in Moscow in the 1960s.

Dawn of the

The Second World War ended in 1945 with the defeat of Germany and Japan. While the victory celebrations were going on, there were also fears for the future. Between 1945 and 1949, the wartime alliance of the United States, Britain and Soviet Russia broke down and a COLD WAR began. This is the name given to the conflict between the USA on one side, and the USSR on the other.

In this Unit you will study the origins of the Cold War and how the world was affected by the start of the age of atomic weapons.

▲ SOURCE 1
The aftermath of the atomic bomb explosion in Hiroshima, 1945.

Key Questions

Why did the USA and the USSR become rivals? Who was more to blame?

How did atomic weapons affect relations between the Great Powers?

How did the USSR gain control of Eastern Europe and how did the USA react?

What were the consequences of the Berlin blockade?

At 8.16 on the morning of 6 August 1945, a US plane dropped an ATOMIC BOMB on the Japanese city of Hiroshima. For American and ALLIED soldiers, it marked the end of one nightmare – the Second World War. However, a new nightmare had begun, not only for the Japanese but also for the rest of the world. This was the age of the atomic bomb – weapons with terrifying destructive power. Little wonder that Robert Oppenheimer, one of the leaders of the Manhattan Project which built these first atom bombs, quoted the words from the Bible: 'I am become death, the shatterer of worlds'.

Why was the atom bomb dropped?
American atomic research was originally aimed at defeating Nazi Germany rather than Japan. But when the war against Germany ended in May 1945, attention turned to ending the war against the stubborn Japanese.

Japanese soldiers had shown that they would fight to the death rather than surrender. The American Joint Chiefs' belief was that any invasion of Japan could take 18 months and cost one million men. The atom bomb, on the other hand, might well bring the war to an end and avoid further loss of

Cold War

atomic age

Investigation

People have different views about the decision to drop the atomic bomb on Hiroshima. The views in Sources 2 and 3 were expressed in 1995.

What is different about these interpretations? Why do people interpret the past differently?

SOURCE 2

Japan really wanted to surrender seeing the incineration of Japanese cities. Although the Japanese leaders wanted to surrender, the Americans wanted to prolong the war because they wanted to use the atomic bomb.

(Professor Mitsuo Okamoto, Hiroshima University.)

SOURCE 3

"The bombs helped to bring an end to the war because when the bombs fell, the army could save face. They were not to blame – it was the technological superiority of the United States, so they could go along with the decision to surrender."

(Professor Kimitada Miwa, Tokyo University.)

life on both sides. When, on 28 July 1945, the Japanese government refused to surrender, President Truman of the USA gave the final go ahead for the use of the bomb. Some people have argued that such a show of American power had other uses, apart from defeating the Japanese. Although the Soviet Union and the USA had been wartime allies, there was concern about how quickly Soviet power was spreading through Europe (see page 8). Stalin, the leader of the USSR, was also preparing to attack Japan, possibly spreading communist influence even further. The bomb would show the USA's power. As Truman put it, 'I'll certainly have a hammer on Stalin'.

Should the bomb have been used at all against a Japanese city? Some of the American scientists were unhappy and argued that a demonstration in an uninhabited area might persuade the Japanese to surrender. However, with only two bombs ready for use, this was seen as too risky.

The Hiroshima fireball

Hiroshima was chosen as the target. On 6 August Lt-Col. Paul Tibbets, the pilot of the B-29 Superfortress (named Enola Gay after his mother), released the bomb they called 'Little Boy'. It detonated 700 metres above the city in a huge devastating flash. A fireball, estimated at 300,000°C, melted metal and stone. People were vaporised to dust and almost every building and person within 1.5 km of the blast was destroyed (Source 1). Survivors wandered about the streets dazed, burned and poisoned by the radiation. 90,000 were killed almost immediately. In the months and years that followed 50,000 more died of the lingering effects of radiation.

Three days after the Hiroshima explosion, a second bomb was dropped on Nagasaki. Five days later Japan surrendered, leaving the USA as the strongest power in the world – stronger than all the other countries put together. The basis of their power was the bomb, but the Soviets were never likely to accept this balance of power. Stalin was eager to get on equal terms and develop his own atomic bomb. The USSR tested its first atom bomb in 1949. A deadly arms race had started. This is what made the Cold War so dangerous. At its height both sides had enough nuclear weapons to blow up the entire world and end all life on this planet. It was a war no one could avoid.

A history of mistrust

1917–1945: The coming of peace or the origins of conflict?

Hitler committed suicide in his Berlin bunker on 30 April 1945. Soviet tanks and soldiers were only a few streets away and the whole of the German capital was soon to be in their hands. Soldiers of the Grand Alliance had been closing in steadily for months – the Russians from the East, the Americans and British from the West. On 7 May Admiral Doenitz signed the paper which marked the German surrender to the Allies; the war in Europe was over.

The urgent task of defeating Hitler's forces had kept this alliance together since 1941. When Soviet and American forces met (Source 4) they were friendly enough but for how long?

Even before the war had ended, there were disagreements between the wartime allies: Britain, the USA and the Soviet Union. Was this so surprising? They had always been uneasy allies, extremely suspicious of each other. Once the common enemy had gone what could hold them together?

Source 5 shows how the Nazis tried to make the Allies jealous of each other. Hitler always hoped he could break up the Allies. Perhaps, he thought, there was a chance that the USSR might end up fighting against Britain and the USA. Why?

◄ SOURCE 4
American and Russian soldiers meet in 1945.

SOURCE 5 ►
A Nazi wartime cartoon showing America making itself rich at the expense of Britain and the Soviet Union.

A clash of ideologies

USSR: A communist system

In the Soviet Union, the COMMUNIST system meant that farms, land, factories and transport were owned by the government and run for the good of the state or country and not for private profit. The Soviet Union was a one-party dictatorship in which Stalin and his communist committees decided how to rule the country. There were no free elections which might lead to a change in the communist hold on power because people could only vote for members of the Communist Party. Stalin could not be voted out of power by the people. The USSR feared the capitalist system and saw American power as a threat. So, it was important to spread the Russian system as widely as possible to counter American power. They did this through the Comintern.

One aim of the Comintern was to encourage the world communist revolution by helping workers and communists in other countries to undermine the capitalist system.

USA: A capitalist system

In the USA and the West, the CAPITALIST system meant that farms, land, transport and factories are owned by private people or companies and run for their own profit.

The USA is a DEMOCRACY with a number of political parties. Free elections decide which people should and should not rule the country. The President could be voted out of power by the people.

The USA and the West saw the communist system as a menace which must not spread to other countries. They were worried by the existence of the Comintern.

> **SOURCE 6**
>
> Perhaps you think that because we are allies of the English, we have forgotten who they are and who Churchill is?
>
> (Stalin complaining during the war about Churchill.)

1917–1921

The Bolsheviks (Communists) took over Russia in 1917. Between 1918 and 1921 there was a civil war as the Bolsheviks tried to hold on to power. Troops from Great Britain and the United States, as well as France and Japan, attempted to destroy the new communist government by sending troops to help the Whites, the enemies of the Communists. Winston Churchill was a noisy supporter of these campaigns against the Bolsheviks (see Source 6).

In the 1930s

Stalin concentrated on 'Socialism in one country' so he paid most attention to building up Russia and, at first, what was happening outside Russia took second place.

But he could not ignore the threat from Hitler's Germany, which was growing more powerful. Nazis looked to Eastern Europe and Russia as areas where they might grab land and make what they said were 'inferior' Slav peoples into slaves.

Britain and France disliked both Hitler and Communist Russia. In the end, Britain failed to get the USSR's help against Germany. Britain and France did nothing to stop Hitler taking over parts of Europe in the 1930s. So Stalin began to think that western European countries were keen for Germany to succeed at the USSR's expense.

In 1939

The Nazi–Soviet Pact was signed. Germany and the USSR agreed not to attack each other. Stalin knew Hitler hated communism. Nevertheless Stalin was keen to avoid war and win some time to build up the USSR's military strength. Britain and France were astonished by the Pact.

Germany and the USSR also agreed to share Poland between themselves. When the USSR also attacked Finland, Britain and France branded the USSR the aggressor; in a final move, the USSR was expelled from the League of Nations. This confirmed what Stalin had always thought – Britain and France would never have made trustworthy allies.

During the Second World War

From 1940 Britain fought Nazi Germany alone until 1941, when Hitler's 'Operation Barbarossa' began the German attack on Soviet Russia. Hitler had torn the Nazi–Soviet Pact up.

The USA was also brought into the war when the Japanese airforce attacked part of the American fleet at Pearl Harbor (1941).

Only a common enemy had forced these three to become allies. How different were their aims and attitudes?

Stalin believed Russia had to be protected at all costs. Soviet wartime losses made grim reading. She suffered at the hands of the German war machine much more than any other country:

- 20 million died.
- 3 million Russians never returned from German labour camps.
- Leningrad and Stalingrad were destroyed at terrible human cost.

Stalin complained bitterly that America and Britain had dragged their feet by not invading Western Europe in 1944 as quickly as they might have done. This would have helped the USSR by opening up another front and diverting German troops from the east. There was little wonder that he was determined to keep the USSR safe from attack after the war.

Assessment

SOURCE 7

The Soviet Union's loss of life (in the war) has been several times greater than that of Britain and the USA put together. Possibly there is a tendency in some quarters to forget the colossal sacrifices of the Soviet people which secured the liberation of Europe from Hitler. But the Soviet Union cannot forget them. And so what can there be surprising about the fact that the Soviet Union, anxious for its future safety, is trying to see that governments loyal to the Soviet Union should exist in neighbouring countries?

(In March 1946, Stalin defended Soviet actions after the war.)

1 *Do you think Table A is more helpful than Table B in explaining why Britain, the Soviet Union and the United States were 'uneasy allies'?*

2 *What did Stalin mean when he said that he had not 'forgotten who Churchill is' (Source 6)?*

3 *Source 7 suggests that Stalin's main concern was with the safety of the Soviet Union. Is this true? Explain your answer.*

Shaping the future

Why were cracks beginning to appear in the Grand Alliance?

How were the attitudes of the 'Big Three' changing as the end of the Second World War came nearer? The two major conferences which were meant to shape the future peace were held at Yalta (in the USSR) and Potsdam (in Germany).

Both conferences took place against the background of a dramatic Soviet expansion into Europe. The Red Army, 6 million strong, was flooding in from the east. The map in Source 8 shows how the countries of Eastern Europe were overrun and fell into the hands of the Red Army. What would the future hold now?

SOURCE 8 ►
The advance of communism in Europe.

Advance of Red Army

Yugoslavia – independent communist state

Iron Curtain

CONFERENCE 1: YALTA, FEBRUARY 1945

▲SOURCE 9
The 'Big Three' at Yalta: Churchill, Roosevelt and Stalin.

What did each side think the other was up to?

Churchill, the British Prime Minister and wartime leader, recognised the danger and wrote to the United States urging that action be taken to stop the USSR's 'onward sweep' (Source 11).

He never trusted Stalin. He did try to get on better with him but admitted it was like trying to deal with a crocodile: 'You do not know whether to tickle it under the chin or to beat it over the head. When it opens its mouth you cannot tell whether it is trying to smile or is preparing to eat you up.' However, Churchill had to be careful. He dare not criticise Stalin too much as the public in Britain had been impressed by Russia's courage and sacrifice against the Nazis.

President Roosevelt (USA):
He regarded Churchill as someone who just wanted to hang on to the British Empire. The United States had no intention of helping Britain in this task. Instead, the aim was to keep the Allies together.

He was keen that all people should be able to choose their own government through free elections, and he wanted a new peace-keeping organisation to be set up after the war. He did his best to get on with Stalin and treat the USSR fairly, much to Churchill's annoyance. Roosevelt fully intended to give Stalin the benefit of the doubt so that the USSR would join the United Nations, the organisation on which Roosevelt pinned many of his hopes of a new world order once the war was over.

Stalin saw things differently and this marks out how much one side failed to understand the other. When the Soviet leader used the words 'free elections' he meant something quite different from Roosevelt. Stalin would never have agreed to the election of non-communists in countries occupied by the Red (Soviet) Army, only elections to elect different members of the Communist Party. He had no intention of leaving the USSR open to attack.

Stalin saw Poland as the route through which the USSR's enemies had passed and here was the opportunity to close this route by creating a buffer between Western Europe and Russia; a buffer of friendly communist states.

Decisions made at Yalta
The 'Big Three' decided to:
1 Divide Germany into four zones of military occupation.
2 Give all the Allies access to the capital, Berlin, which was in the Soviet zone. So it too was divided into four sectors of military occupation (see Source 18).
3 Make Germany pay reparations.
4 Bring Nazi war criminals to trial.
5 Allow elections so that the peoples of Eastern Europe could choose their new governments democratically.
6 Sign a charter to set up a United Nations organisation.

In addition the USSR agreed to declare war on Japan 'in the next three months' and help defeat her.

Following the Yalta conference . . .
• Germany was defeated.
• So was Churchill but in a General Election. The new Prime Minister was Clement Attlee.
• Roosevelt died and his place as President was taken by Harry Truman.

Europe in ruins

The human cost of the war was bad enough: estimates of war dead in Europe alone stood at over 30 million. Cities had been reduced to mountains of rubble. Millions of refugees had lost their homes. In Cologne, for example, people lived in the cellars of bombed houses, and fetched their water from the few pumps which had survived. People returned to the city to find their homes in ruins. There was no gas, electricity or transport.

Shortage of food was the most urgent problem (Source 10), and the Allies were not equal to the job of feeding the huge numbers of half-starved refugees who roamed central Europe. Money was worthless and cigarettes became the only currency many people would accept. With communications destroyed and farms and factories devastated, the outlook was bleak.

▲ SOURCE 10
Two German boys try to find something to eat in rubbish left by the British, 1945.

In what ways did American attitudes change?

There were soon complaints about the stripping of industrial wealth from Germany. It was being loaded on to trains bound for the Soviet Union. One American wrote bitterly of '17 million Germans living under Red Army occupation virtually in slavery'.

And then there was the key issue of Poland. What had happened about Article 5 of the Yalta agreement (see box on page 8)? The new President of the USA, Harry Truman, suspected that Stalin had never intended to allow countries under communist control the freedom to hold democratic elections. Stalin would ensure that only communists were in control. During the spring of 1945, the USSR was busy setting up 'puppet' governments in several countries, particularly Poland.

British attitudes too were hardening. In 1939 Britain had declared war to defend Poland's freedom from German fascism. In 1945 who was now defending Poland from communist control?

In the weeks following Yalta these cracks in the Grand Alliance were just beginning to appear. However, all was not lost; as a gesture to Stalin, American troops left the Soviet zone. Truman did not want Stalin to think that the other allies were ganging up on the USSR.

The American President knew that further help was needed to defeat Japan, so the alliance had to be kept intact. Despite Churchill's warnings in Source 11, Truman still wanted to try and settle things in a friendly way with the Russians. Would this spirit continue as the leaders moved onto to the next conference at Potsdam?

SOURCE 11

"The Soviet Union has become a danger to the free world. A new front must be created against her onward sweep. This front in Europe should be as far East as possible . . . A settlement must be reached on all major issues between the West and East in Europe before the armies of democracy melt."

(Churchill speaking in 1945.)

QUESTIONS

1 How can the map (Source 8) help you to explain the problems facing Churchill, Roosevelt and Stalin at Yalta?

2 How did the USSR gain control of so much of Eastern Europe?

3 Explain how Stalin might have replied to the attitude shown in Source 11.

From Potsdam to containment

Truman, so far, seemed to have under-estimated what Churchill saw as the threat from Soviet Russia. Stalin continued to strengthen the communist position in Eastern Europe and, thereby, the defence of the USSR. The next conference, held at Potsdam in July 1945, did little to help each side understand the other.

Of the original Big Three only Stalin was left. Truman personally disliked Stalin so was pleased when an American adviser told him to 'stop babying the Soviets'. Advice like that could lead to conflict. Truman, however, still wanted to settle matters peacefully.

The leaders left Potsdam with the future looking bleak. Uppermost in people's minds was the American atomic bomb. Stalin had been told of its planned use only 11 days before Hiroshima. Truman made it clear that he would not share the new technology wth the USSR, a decision Stalin was never going to accept.

Stalin thought he now had even more reason to fear the US. Why had the weapon been kept such a secret when they were all supposed to be allies? Henry Stimson, the US Secretary for War, wrote to Truman in September 1945 and explained that unless the USA talked to the Soviets about the bomb 'their suspicions and their distrust of our motives will increase'.

Containment in action

In 1946 President Truman went to Fulton, Missouri where he listened to a speech by Winston Churchill. This speech repeated earlier warnings about the threat from Moscow. It called for an alliance against the Soviet Union (Source 12).

> ## SOURCE 12
>
> A shadow has fallen upon the scenes so lately lighted by the Allied victory. Nobody knows what Soviet Russia intends to do in the immediate future or what are the limits to their expansive tendencies. From Stettin on the Baltic to Trieste on the Adriatic, an iron curtain has descended across the Continent. Behind that line lie all the capitals of Central and Eastern Europe . . . and all are subject to a very high measure of control from Moscow.
>
> (From Winston Churchill's 'Iron Curtain' speech, Fulton, Missouri, 5 March 1946.)

CONFERENCE 2: POTSDAM, JULY 1945

At the conference:

• The decision made at Yalta to split Germany and Berlin between the four occupying powers was once again agreed.
• Austria was to be separate from Germany but under joint occupation.
• Germany would be run by an Allied Control Commission; the four military commanders of the occupying armies would sit on this.

• Germany would be denazified and trials of war criminals would go ahead at Nuremberg.
• Reparations could be taken by each occupying power from its own zone, although the USSR would be allowed to take some industrial goods from the American and British zones. The reparations could not be so severe as to endanger ordinary people's lives.
• No further talks took place about the future of Germany.

SOURCE 13 ▶
Cartoon drawn by a Soviet artist, 1948. The words underneath the cartoon read: 'Defenders of Greece. Forward, Your Country Needs You.'

At first Truman did not agree with Churchill. But by 1947 he was beginning to share Churchill's views. The USSR was keen to expand into the Mediterranean and the Middle East. In response, the US Sixth Fleet was sent to the Black Sea to persuade the Soviets to remove their soldiers from the area to the north of the oil fields of Iran. The arms race continued.

In February 1947 the British told the Americans that they could no longer keep sending arms and support to the Greek government. Since 1944 Britain had been helping the Greek King fight communist GUERRILLAS for control of the country (see Source 13). Britain, struggling with a terrible winter, power cuts and trying to pay off crippling wartime debts, was no longer in a position to help. Nor could it help Turkey, also under threat.

How would the USA react? Would it return to isolation and leave Europe to sort out its own problems? Or would the USA take the huge step and commit itself as the major power in the Mediterranean?

The crucial decisions were taken by three men: the President, his Secretary of State General George Marshall and, most importantly, by Dean Acheson, who worked for Marshall. Acheson was the one who gave American foreign policy a vital push. He did not want Greece, Turkey and the oil states of the Middle East to be like 'apples in a barrel – infected by the rotten one'.

The Truman Doctrine
On 12 March 1947 Truman made a speech in Congress (Source 14). The ideas in it became known as the Truman Doctrine. In the speech Truman stated that the USA's aim was to stop communist expansion all over the world. Was this the declaration of a Cold War? Or was it just a defensive move to contain communism within existing boundaries? It was a dramatic move. Some have called it a revolution in American foreign policy. Yet it was not popular with everyone in the USA. Truman was accused of starting 'a century of fear'.

In the end there was little opposition to Truman. Congress gave US$400 million to Greece and Turkey immediately, and the communist threat in Greece was eventually defeated.

SOURCE 14

I believe that it must be the policy of the United States to support free peoples who are resisting attempted SUBJUGATION by armed minorities or by outside pressures.

I believe that we must assist free peoples to work out their own destinies in their own way.

(The 'Truman Doctrine', 12 March 1947.)

◄ SOURCE 15
Cartoon from *Punch*, a British magazine, published in October 1947.

NEIGHBOURS

"Come on, Sam! It's up to us again."

Assessment

1 *What is meant by the term 'Iron Curtain'? In what ways was it 'iron'? In what ways was it a curtain?*

2 *One historian has said that the Cold War began in 1947. How accurate is this view? Explain your answer.*

3 *In what ways are the Soviet cartoon (Source 13) and the **Punch** cartoon (Source 15) biased sources of information about the Truman Doctrine.*

4 *Does the fact that these cartoons put forward a point of view mean that they are no use as evidence? Explain your answer.*

5 *In what ways does the Truman Doctrine mark a change in US foreign policy?*

Marshall Aid

The other half of the Truman Doctrine was Marshall Aid. Soviet power would remain a threat as long as Europe was weak. Europe was indeed giving real cause for concern: famine, disease, a terrible winter (1947), weak governments, homelessness and production below pre-war levels. Marshall was a man of great humanity, arguing that 'our policy is directed not against country or doctrine, but against hunger, poverty, desperation and chaos'. However, he was also motivated by more than generosity: 'The seeds [of communism] spread and grow in the evil soil of poverty.'

Strong action was needed as the governments of France and Italy were under threat from local communist parties. Marshall therefore put forward a plan to spend billions of dollars to help the shattered nations of Europe recover, so they could defend themselves against communism. As one historian has shown, the Marshall Plan 'did prevent the shadow of the Kremlin from darkening the entire Continent'.

Dollar aid – the communist interpretation
By the beginning of 1948 the Marshall Plan was in place. Billions of dollars would help Europe to rebuild itself. Aid was also offered to countries behind the Iron Curtain.

Did the Americans really expect Stalin to agree to the distribution of Marshall Aid to eastern Europe? Whatever the answer, Stalin would have nothing to do with it; he thought it would give the USA the chance to have a say in what was happening behind the 'Iron Curtain'. Stalin accused the Americans of economic IMPERIALISM: spreading their influence and using dollars to bribe Europe into uniting against the USSR.

To the Soviet Union, the USA was using its economic power to further dominate Europe and threaten the safety and defence of the Russian people. The Russians wasted no time in using its veto at the United Nations to stop any attempt to weaken the Soviet position. The American menace would have to be defeated by forming new organisations.

In 1947 the Cominform (Communist

The Marshall Plan: Factfile

- Between 1948 and 1952 $13,150 million was given to 16 European countries.
- Most went to Britain and France.
- Europe worked together to plan and use the money, setting up the Organisation for European Economic Co-operation (OEEC).
- At first the money went on food, animal feed and fertilisers to raise agricultural production.
- Later on, dollar aid stimulated the production of machinery, vehicles and fuel.
- Marshall Aid was offered to the USSR and its communist SATELLITES.
- Stalin refused to accept this offer.

⬛ SOURCE 16
'Yankee Go Home.' A communist poster attacking the Marshall Plan.

SOURCE 17
The Americans said that the Marshall Plan was 'a plan to save peace'. This was not true. It was really intended to unite countries against the Soviet Union. The USA hoped that it would lead to a split among the communist states and bring them under American influence. It was also clear that the Marshall Plan aimed to rebuild the military power of Western Germany.

(From *Soviet Foreign Policy*, written in 1968 by I. S. Kremer, a Soviet historian.)

Information Bureau) was set up to help European communist parties work together more closely and co-operate about tactics. Later, in 1949, Comecon (the Council for Mutual Economic Aid) was set up to encourage economic co-operation between the communist states.

The position of Berlin

While the Second World War was being fought, the Allies had concentrated on the defeat of Hitler, without agreeing what they might do with Germany once they had won. It was only when the Big Three met at Yalta and Potsdam that decisions were taken to divide Germany between the Americans, British, French and Russians. Source 18 shows not only this division, but also the awkward situation of Berlin, deep in the Soviet zone, it too divided between the four victorious powers. Much depended on the goodwill of the Soviets to allow free passage, by land, of supplies to the French, British and American sectors of Berlin.

Under Marshall Aid, dollars were also beginning to flood into the three western zones of Germany as well as the western sectors of Berlin. To the Soviets, it seemed as if the former wartime enemy was being strengthened and the lines marking out the communist east from the areas controlled by Britain, France and the USA were being drawn in more clearly.

The West decided they could not let the German people starve. The best way of preventing this was to allow some German economic recovery. To Stalin and the Russians, this was out of the question (Source 19).

The battle over currency

In 1948, the British and Americans met in London to discuss the future of Germany. No Russian was present. It was agreed that Germany needed a new currency. Germans could not buy and sell goods with any confidence unless they had money that would not lose its value. When the Soviets asked for a report of the meeting, the request was turned down. To Stalin this meeting was the last straw. Within hours, a dangerous chain of events had started.

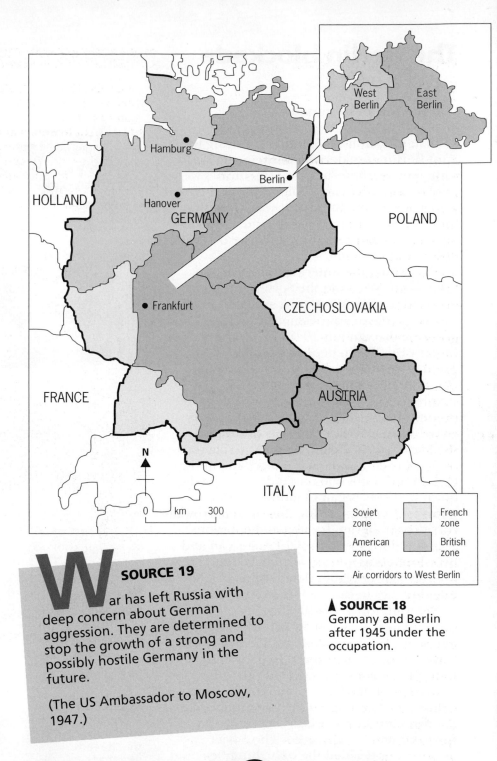

SOURCE 18
Germany and Berlin after 1945 under the occupation.

SOURCE 19
War has left Russia with deep concern about German aggression. They are determined to stop the growth of a strong and possibly hostile Germany in the future.

(The US Ambassador to Moscow, 1947.)

QUESTIONS

1 'The Soviet Union was right to feel threatened by the Truman Doctrine and Marshall Plan.' How far do you agree with this statement?

2 How does Source 16 help us to understand the Marshall Plan?

3 Source 17 is another, later, interpretation of the Marshall Plan. How do you explain this historian's views? Use the source and other knowledge to help you explain your answer.

The Berlin blockade and airlift

Why was the airlift started?

At first, in March 1948, trains travelling to West Berlin were delayed by the Soviets and some were turned back. British convoys were held up at Soviet checkpoints. Then, the road bridge across the River Elbe was 'closed for repairs'. By 24 June 1948, all land routes to West Berlin had been blocked. The blockade of Berlin had begun.

What would the Americans, British and French do? What did the Soviets intend to do? Had they meant to turn an incident into a crisis? Truman was pessimistic, writing in his personal diary in July 1948, 'We are very close to war'. But Berlin needed supplies. As Truman would not shoot his way into the city, the only alternative was an airlift.

Nobody knew if it would be possible to keep two million Berliners supplied by air. They would need at least 4,000 tons of supplies such as food, fuel, clothing and medicines a day. In the early days of the blockade, things looked bad. Only 600 tons a day were being flown in. Costs began to mount as Allied pilots felt their way along the three narrow air corridors to Berlin. Ice, fog and collisions accounted for the lives of 79 American and British pilots as well as German ground crew. Russian fighter planes flew alarmingly close to Allied planes in case any strayed off course. As the winter of 1948–1949 arrived, the Russians cut off electricity supplies although they tried to bribe people with the promise of extra rations if they moved to their eastern sector. Few, only 2%, accepted the 'offer'. In one incident, the US commander in Berlin retaliated by cutting off the gas supply (which ran through the American sector) to the Soviet commander's house. The Soviet commander decided the only thing he could do was to move house, but when he tried to move his furniture through the American sector, it was seized by the US Army.

In April 1949, 1,400 planes landed in a single day in West Berlin – a record. The daily average delivered rose to 8,000 tons a day. Frank Donovan, who took part in the airlift, wrote of the 'glittering belt of aircraft', flying 90 seconds apart. While it had proved possible for West Berlin to survive, how long would it all last?

◄ **SOURCE 20**
'The Birdwatcher', cartoon by E. H. Shepard for *Punch* magazine, July 1948.

> ## SOURCE 21
>
> Father said, 'They're actually doing it! They're flying food to Berlin. But they won't be able to bring in enough. Think of this huge city!'
>
> The first package of POM [dried potatoes]. It was like a magic show. Will it really turn into something or will it all be lumpy? 'It's getting thick! Look!', cried Frau Schultze, and the first dehydrated potato soup with mother's green vegetables tasted wonderful to all of us.
>
> (An eye-witness remembered the early days of the airlift.)

SOURCE 22 ►
A German child drew this. It reads 'We thank the pilots for their work and efforts.'

SOURCE 23

When we refused to be forced out of Berlin, we showed Europe that we would act when freedom was threatened. This action was a Russian plan to probe the soft spots in the Western Allies' positions.

(Truman's view, written in his *Memoirs*, 1955.)

SOURCE 24

The crisis was planned in Washington, behind a smoke-screen of anti-Soviet propaganda. The conduct of the Western powers risked bloody incidents. The self-blockade of the Western powers hit the West Berlin population with harshness. The people were freezing and starving. In 1949, the USA was forced to yield . . . their war plans had come to nothing.

(This was the Russian view.)

The end of the blockade

Neither side was prepared to give in. Talks began in secret in February 1949 and the blockade ended in May, after 11 months (see Source 25). West Berlin had survived. But the fate of Germany was sealed for the next 40 years. The eastern part of the city remained in communist hands.

In May the former British, French and US zones were combined to form the Federal Republic of West Germany (including West Berlin, where the three sectors had been AMALGAMATED). The Federal Republic was closely linked to the West. On the other side of the Iron Curtain, the German Democratic Republic, a separate communist state, was formed in October.

NATO

A re-united Germany seemed out of the question. Even before the end of the blockade the North Atlantic Treaty Organisation (NATO) had been formed by 12 Western countries, who wanted a defensive shield against communist attack. The Soviet Union saw NATO as a threat.

For the time being, conflict had been avoided because talks had settled the crisis. As one historian commented: 'the Cold War would never be so hot in Europe again'.

◀ SOURCE 25
The first lorry for 300 days reaches West Berlin.

Assessment

1 What evidence is there in these sources that the people of Berlin were determined to survive the blockade?

2 Sources 23 and 24 are discussing the same event. In what ways are the sources different in their assessment of the Berlin blockade?

3 What problems would a historian have studying these two sources? What other information might help a historian come to a conclusion about which side was to blame for the blockade?

Two great nations

In Unit 1 we saw how the wartime anti-German alliance of the USSR and USA broke down after 1945, and how a 'Cold War' began in Europe. It became clear soon after the war that the USA and USSR were much more powerful than any other country. They had become 'superpowers'. In this Unit we shall look at the beliefs and actions of both these superpowers. We shall also see how the Cold War became a global conflict.

Key Questions

What is a superpower?

How did the people in each superpower live?

How did the superpowers use their strength?

How did the Cold War become worldwide?

Before the Second World War there were no SUPERPOWERS. Instead there were several strong European nations – Britain, Germany, France – made even stronger by wealth from their overseas empires.

The war changed everything. After six years of fighting, the nations of Europe were weak and exhausted. They faced serious problems: millions of people had been killed; homes and communications were damaged; trade was almost at a standstill; millions of refugees had to be fed and sheltered. Elsewhere in the world, nations that had once been European colonies were demanding their independence. Sometimes this was achieved peacefully. More often, as in Algeria or Indo-China, independence was only won after years of fighting.

These 'COLONIAL wars' further weakened the power of European nations. As well as the cost in manpower and machinery, the end of empires also led to a loss of income, influence and prestige.

The rise of the superpowers
'Superpower' was a good description for both the USA and the USSR. No other countries could equal them.

◄ SOURCE 1
'Freedom from want', an illustration by the popular American artist, Norman Rockwell.

▲ SOURCE 2
A Soviet poster praising the happiness of family life under communism.

▲ SOURCE 3
'Europe caught in the nuclear crossfire', cartoon by Jim Borgman, 1982.

Both were vast in size. Together, they covered over 30 million square kilometres – that is, 21 per cent of the Earth's dry surface. Together, their peoples made up 25 per cent of the world's population in 1985. They both had rich resources of fertile farmland, and valuable raw materials for industrial use. Most important of all, for many years they alone had the power to destroy each other – and, if they chose, everyone else on Earth – with nuclear weapons of many different kinds.

Different or similar?

In many ways, the superpowers were very different. They had different political systems and different ideologies (sets of beliefs), and their governments had many different problems to solve at home and abroad. You can find out about all these differences in the rest of this Unit. But in two important ways, the superpowers were very similar, too.

Firstly, both superpowers were proud and full of certainty that their own way of life was the best. They both also wanted to persuade other people that their way of life was the best for them too

Look at Sources 1 and 2. They were both designed to send a message to ordinary men and women in the Russian or American streets. They both reflect confident and powerful visions of what the 'good life' ought to be.

Secondly, both superpowers generated strong feelings among peoples in the rest of the world. Sometimes, they were feelings of admiration for the superpowers' strength and achievements, and of gratitude for their help or protection. But sometimes they were feelings of hatred or fear. Look at Source 3. It shows a newspaper cartoon, drawn in 1982, after the superpowers had been engaged in the Cold War for almost 37 years. What does it tell us about how some smaller, weaker nations saw the mighty superpowers?

The superpowers at home

What was the situation in each nation in the years following the end of the war in 1945?

The USA and the USSR had both fought to defeat Hitler's evil regime. The USSR was invaded by Germany, and ordinary Russian people suffered terribly and fought heroically to defend their homeland. By contrast, most American people suffered very little, although many American troops were killed in action. Japanese bombers attacked American bases in the Pacific, but the American mainland remained entirely untouched by war.

USA: Wages and prices

In the USA, after the war there were protests and strikes by workers in the car, steel and railway industries. Manufacturing had been strictly controlled by the US government during the war; now workers wanted higher wages. High prices charged for basic foodstuffs and for 'luxury' consumer goods caused dangerous inflation. Eggs, for example, rose in price from 33 cents a dozen in 1940 (just before the USA joined in the war) to 72 cents a dozen in 1948, an increase of over 100 per cent.

There was unemployment and social tensions, too. Many returning soldiers found it hard to find a job. Black soldiers, who had fought bravely alongside white American troops, faced particular problems. Racial discrimination was still widespread in many American states. American women also felt disadvantaged. They had worked hard in wartime, in factories, offices and farms. Now the government – and many battle-weary ex-soldiers – wanted women to leave their jobs, forget their new skills, and go back home to devote themselves to domestic chores, by becoming full-time wives and mothers again.

USSR: A shattered land

In the USSR, the problems were far worse. About 20 million Russian citizens had died during the war, over 10 per cent of the population. Around 70,000 villages and almost 2,000 cities and towns had been destroyed. Factories had been devastated, and tens of thousands of farms had been wrecked. Many millions of people were homeless, hungry and without a job.

The Russian leader, Joseph Stalin, was nearing the end of his life (he died in 1953), and was growing ever more ruthless in his determination to keep hold of power. He awarded himself grandiose titles like 'Greatest Genius in History', and anyone who dared to criticise him soon 'disappeared'. (You can read more about this on page 30). All the MEDIA were strictly CENSORED, and there were secret police everywhere. Ordinary citizens were forbidden to travel outside the USSR, or even to make contact with anyone living abroad.

▲ **SOURCE 4**
Heavy industry being rebuilt in the USSR under a new Five-Year Plan started in 1946.

SOURCE 5

"We must help people to live well, dress well and eat well. You cannot put theory in your soup. . . . If after 40 years of communism a person cannot have a glass of milk or a pair of shoes he will not believe communism is a good idea, whatever you tell him.

(Nikita Khrushchev, Soviet leader 1953–1964.)"

Rise to superpower

At first glance, both the USA and the USSR might seem to have been in a terrible mess in the years just after the end of the Second World War. But compared with all other nations, they were still potential 'superpowers'. What strengths did they have that the rest of the world did not? How did they both rebuild their nations and emerge as superpowers?

- They both possessed vast resources of land.
- They both had large populations and lots of workers.
- They both owned valuable natural resources: water, timber, petrol, iron, and coal.
- They both invested in education, science and technology. In the USA, the government passed the 'GI Bill', giving grants to ex-soldiers who wanted to go to college. In the USSR education was free for everyone.
- They rebuilt their damaged economies, although in very different ways.

Stalin made developing the USSR's heavy industry a top priority (Source 4). At the time of his death, in 1953, the USSR was the second most important industrial power in the world, after the USA.

American industry also developed rapidly. But it was run by private enterprise, encouraged by government policies, rather than through state control. The goods manufactured were different, too. Like the Russians, the Americans made locomotives, heavy lorries, farm tractors and mining machines. But American factories also made mass-market consumer goods, from food-mixers and televisions to family cars (Sources 6 and 7). All of these were unheard-of luxuries for ordinary Russian people at that time.

- Both the USA and the USSR built up immensely powerful armies and navies, equipped with the latest weapons, including nuclear bombs. This was very expensive, but provided millions of jobs in engineering, electronics, manufacturing and technology-based industry. These jobs, and the spending-power they gave their employees, encouraged Russian and American economies to grow.
- Last but not least, each nation developed a distinctive 'IDEOLOGY' – a set of beliefs that it used to inspire its own citizens, and to give it a confident sense of superiority when dealing with the rest of the world.

▲ **SOURCE 6**
American cars were built for comfort, luxury and family use. A magazine advertisement for Pontiac cars, 1950.

How did the superpowers recover from war-damage to become more powerful than other nations in the post-war world?

SOURCE 7

The average gross income per family was $4,444 in 1950 and by 1960 had reached $6,819. That is not to say that America did not have her underprivileged citizens in the 1950s, but most people found them easy to ignore. There were other things to think about – like bingo, 3-D movies, TV quiz shows, and newer and gaudier automobiles and home appliances. People were spending a smaller fraction of their income than ever before on the basic necessities of life, such as food and clothes, and rather more than they had ever done on luxuries. And those luxuries included many items – such as television sets, cars, vacations in distant but fashionable places, and subscriptions to glossy weekly magazines – that both extended and were partly promoted by the conformist tastes of the day.

(Written by the British historian Daniel Snowman in 1968.)

In 1954, the USA had . . .

6% of world population

60% of all cars

58% of all telephones

45% of all radio sets

34% of all railways

Friends and enemies

'Containment' or 'conquest'?

By 1949, relations between the new superpowers were tense. As you discovered on pages 10 to 15, the USA and USSR had already come close to war over the future of Berlin, over Stalin's bid to control Poland, Hungary and Czechoslovakia, and over the civil war between communists and royalists in Greece.

These political tensions were reinforced by an increasingly bitter 'war of words'. For over a century, the USA had been devoted to a free-enterprise, capitalist way of life, while the USSR continued to be inspired by Russia's communist revolution of 1917. (Look back at Table A on page 6.) You can also see examples of propaganda generated by this communist/capitalist ideological conflict in the fact box on page 21.

Leaders of both superpowers also made clear declarations about their government's aims. US President Truman set out the future shape of American foreign policy in his famous 'Truman Doctrine' speech of 1947 (Source 8). In response, Stalin's close colleagues, like Beria, made equally vigorous statements setting out the USSR's point of view (Source 9).

▼ **SOURCE 10**
President Truman signing the NATO Treaty, 1949.

SOURCE 8

At the present moment our nation must choose between alternative ways of life. The choice is too often not a free one. Our way of life is based on the free will of the majority, free elections, freedom of speech and freedom from political oppression. . . .

The second way of life is based on the will of a minority forcibly imposed on the majority. It relies on terror and oppression, a controlled press and radio, fixed elections. . . .

I believe that it must be the policy of the USA to support the free peoples who are resisting attempted subjugation by armed minorities and outside pressure.

(Speech by President Harry S. Truman, March 1947.)

SOURCE 9

Stalin has laid down a programme of action for Communists. They must:
(1) exploit all differences and contradictions in the BOURGEOIS camp;
(2) take concrete action to unite the working classes of the economically advanced countries with the national liberation movement in the colonies and dependent nations;
(3) complete the struggle for the unity of the Trade Union movement
(4) take active measures to bring together the proletariat [i.e. workers in the cities] and the small peasants;
(5) support Soviet rule and disrupt attacks by imperialists against the Soviet Union, bearing in mind that the Soviet Union is the base of revolutionary movement in all countries.

(Article in the Russian government newspaper, *Pravda*, written by Lavrenti Beria, to celebrate Stalin's 70th birthday, 1950.)

Ideological differences

'West European and American culture is putrid in its moral foundations. The entire host of writers, film-makers and theatrical producers strives to shift the attention of the advanced elements in society from political and social questions into the channel of vulgar and empty art, crowded with gangsters, chorus girls, praise of adultery, and the affairs of adventurers and rogues of every kind.'

Comment by Andrei Zhdanov, Communist leader in Leningrad (St Petersburg), 1946. Zhdanov was a member of the Politburo, the top policy-making committee in the USSR.

'Few would doubt that the past dynamism of our nation has genuinely stemmed from a profound popular faith in such concepts as justice and righteousness and from the sense that our nation had a mission to promote these ideals by every peaceful means. Soviet communism reflects a view totally different from the United States historic view. Its creed is materialistic and ATHEISTIC. It does not admit of any moral law.'

From a speech by John Foster Dulles, shortly before he was appointed Secretary of State (a leading American government post) in 1953.

▲ **SOURCE 11**
A meeting of Comecon, the Soviet economic organisation.

QUESTIONS

1 What would the USA claim was the aim of NATO? What would Stalin say about it?

2 What would Stalin say was the aim of Comecon? What would the USA say about it?

Truman's and Beria's words may seem straightforward, but what did they really mean? Even at the time, they were controversial. From each speaker's view, their government was aiming at 'CONTAINMENT'. That is, each superpower wanted to defend what it already had, 'contain' its rival and support its friends. But, from the rival superpower's point of view, this 'support' looked liked a threat. Both the USA and USSR feared that the other wanted to **conquer** the world.

Making friends
Although they found themselves opposed to one another, neither the USSR nor the USA really wanted war. So they tried to make themselves stronger through a system of alliances. You can see these on the map on page 27. In 1949, NATO (the North Atlantic Treaty Organisation) was established (Source 10). Founder members were Belgium, Canada, Denmark, France, Britain, Iceland, Italy, Luxembourg, the Netherlands, Norway, Portugal and the USA. Greece, Turkey, West Germany and Spain joined later on.

Not to be outdone, the USSR set up Comecon (the Council for Mutual Economic Assistance) in the same year (see Source 11). In 1955 the USSR and its allies formed a military alliance, known as the Warsaw Pact.

There were other alliances, too. SEATO (the South-East Asia Treaty Organisation) was founded in 1954. It allied the USA with Australia, New Zealand, Thailand, the Philippines, Pakistan, Britain and France. The Baghdad Pact, made at first in 1955 between anti-communist Turkey and Iraq, was later joined by Britain, Pakistan, Iran and the USA.

Uneasy balance
As a result of these alliances, and of the propaganda war, by 1949 the world was in a state of nervous, suspicious peace. Leaders in both superpowers spoke of 'spheres of influence' – that is, lands which they did not rule, but over which they had considerable power. Could this uneasy balance be maintained, or would one of the superpowers forget the notion of 'containment' and make a bid to rule the whole world?

Why did the superpowers become involved in Korea?

Since 1910, the remote Far Eastern nation of Korea had been ruled by Japan. The Koreans had tried to overthrow their Japanese conquerors several times, but without success.

Allies and invaders

During the Second World War, the USA and the USSR fought as allies to defeat the Japanese. In 1945, Russian troops invaded Korea from the north. Soon afterwards, American troops invaded Korea from the south. The Koreans were overjoyed. The world's strongest nations were working together to help liberate their land. Still fighting fiercely against the Japanese, the two invading armies marched on until finally they met, face to face. The Japanese were defeated, but, sadly, Korea's problems were not over.

In 1946, the Americans and Russians held talks to decide what to do next. But they could not agree. Was Korea to be ruled by a new government that was friendly to the communists in the Soviet Union, or was it to be ruled by Korean friends and allies of the USA? While the politicians were still debating, two separate governments were established in Korea. In the north, Kim Il Sung set up a strict communist regime; in the south, Syngman Rhee set up a capitalist government which sympathised with the USA.

In 1948, Soviet troops withdrew from North Korea, and in 1949, the Americans withdrew from the south. But Korea was still divided. In 1950, Syngman Rhee, leader of the south, threatened to invade the north. To defend his land (or so he said) northern leader Kim Il Sung launched a real invasion of the south in June. He was probably acting on Stalin's advice. The world, looking on, was shocked. Here were communists and capitalists in open conflict. Was this the beginning of the third world war?

Invasion

The Americans were quick to act. By 1 July they sent troops to support South Korea (Source 13). The poster image in Source 15

and the comment by US General MacArthur (Source 14) explain why. The victory of the Communists in China in 1949, and the USSR's atom bomb test, also in 1949, led many Americans to think they were losing the Cold War. The USA called on the United Nations to oppose the invasion. The USSR was boycotting the UN at the time, so an armed UN force was put together by several nations, including Britain. The joint force advanced rapidly through North Korea. But when it approached the Chinese border, a new crisis loomed. The Chinese communist government threatened to join in the fight, on the side of the North Koreans.

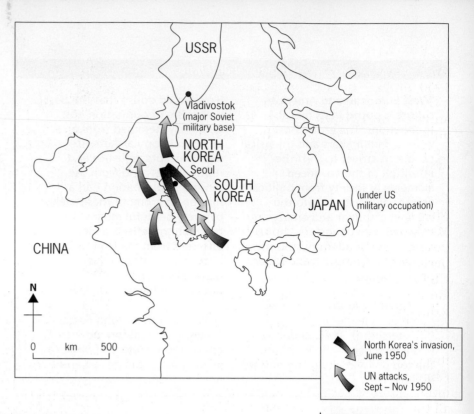

▲ **SOURCE 12**
Korea and the influence of the superpowers in the Far East and Pacific.

▼ **SOURCE 13**
UN troops, led by General Douglas MacArthur, landing at Pohang, 7 July 1950.

The Chinese finally invaded in November 1950, pushing the UN troops back.

During all this fighting, Korean troops and civilians suffered severely. Between 3 and 4 million people were killed, and there were severe food shortages and outbreaks of disease.

Ceasefire

After the Chinese invasion, General MacArthur wanted to launch a full-scale invasion, to 'liberate' Korea completely and perhaps China from communist rule. But US President Truman was more cautious. He stayed true to his declared policy of 'containment'. Conquest of communist rivals was not part of his plan. Truman dismissed General MacArthur in 1951, and this gesture reassured the Russians and Chinese. They believed that Truman did not want to provoke another world war. So all three powers – USA, USSR and China – agreed to a ceasefire in November 1951. In 1953, a 'peace line' was established along the border between North and South Korea (Source 16). They still remain two separate nations today.

Further alliances

Korea had given both superpowers great cause for concern. They had gone to the brink of another conflict, which threatened to engulf the whole world. But they were determined, if possible, to keep the Cold War 'cold', and stop it 'hotting up' into a full-blown war. So they did what they could to enlarge their 'spheres of influence' by peaceful means, through making more alliances. You can read about the most important of them on page 21.

SOURCE 14

Asia is where the communist conspirators have elected to make their play for global conquest. If we lose this war to communism in Asia, the fall of Europe is inevitable. There is no substitute for victory.

(Comment by General Douglas MacArthur, commander of US forces in the Korean War.)

◄ SOURCE 15
A US propaganda poster about the communist threat to Korea and the Far East, 1950.

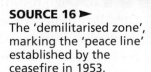

SOURCE 16 ►
The 'demilitarised zone', marking the 'peace line' established by the ceasefire in 1953.

Assessment

1 **Make a timeline of the history of Korea from 1945 to 1953**

2 **What did Truman and MacArthur disagree about?**

3 **What were the results of the Korean War: For the Cold War? For Korea?**

Communist China

Since 1937 and during the Second World War, China had been fighting against the Japanese invaders. Before this there had been many years of civil war.

After 1945 civil war flared up between the Nationalist Chinese and the Communists (led by Mao Zedong). It finally ended in victory for Mao and the Communists.

A new nation, the People's Republic of China, was founded in 1949. Like the USSR and USA it was vast, with rich resources and a huge population. But it was too busy sorting out its own problems at home to aim for world power. And although China had a large army, it was no rival for the superpowers. Nor did it have a nuclear bomb in 1949.

Suspicion

In this Unit we will look at relations between the superpowers during the 1950s and 1960s.

These were tense decades in the Cold War. Both sides built up their armed forces and nuclear weapons. Some people on both sides objected to the Cold War: we shall see what happened to them. We shall also see how the two sides became involved in the crisis which came nearest to nuclear war: the Cuban Missile Crisis.

SOURCE 1 ►
The superpower threat viewed from each side. A cartoon by Ingram Pinn from *The Sunday Times*.

Key Questions

What were the superpowers' aims during the 1950s and 1960s?

How did these aims affect the rest of the world?

What was 'the balance of power'?

How real was the danger of nuclear war in this period?

Many people who lived through the era of the Cold War look back and remember two powerful feelings from that time: suspicion and fear. Suspicion arose because neither the USA nor the USSR really understood the other. Each felt hostile to the other's ideology, and unable to trust anything the other's leaders said. Both superpowers also went to great lengths to keep important information about themselves top secret. For example, no-one knew how many nuclear missiles the USSR had, or how many bombs and bombers the USA had hidden away.

To make matters worse, both superpowers actively spread 'misinformation' about themselves and each other through the world's media, to make it harder for anyone to discover what the true situation was. It is easy to see how this secrecy led to exaggerated suspicions in both superpowers. What does Source 1 tell us about the USA's and the USSR's worries and fears?

A show of power
Rival superpower leaders, like US President Kennedy and the Soviet leader Khrushchev

and fear

▲ **SOURCE 2**
Nikita Khrushchev and J. F. Kennedy. ▶

(Source 2), faced a difficult task. Neither wanted outright war; it was in both superpowers' interests to spend time and money developing farming, industry and technology at home. But the leaders of both superpowers also had to maintain the 'balance of power'. They could not afford to let their own country appear weak in the face of the threat from the rival superpower.

This rivalry led to an expensive 'arms race', as each side built up its weapons and invented new ones. All over the world capitalism and communism, the USA and the USSR faced each other, unwilling to back down.

The rest of the world
Suspicion and fear were not confined to the superpowers. Most people who lived through the 1950s and 1960s would have agreed with the view of South Korean leader, Syngman Rhee, recorded in Source 3.

It seemed impossible that communist USSR and capitalist USA could exist peacefully side by side. Surely, one of them would soon attack the other? The whole world seemed to be balanced on the edge of global war.

> **SOURCE 3**
> We are all caught up in a gigantic global struggle between communism and democracy. Co-existence of these two ideologies is impossible. Either one or the other must go. This is the great and tragic historical fact that our generation must face and understand.
>
> Syngman Rhee, leader of anti-communist South Korea, 1950.

War or peace?

Looking back at the 1950s and 1960s today, we know now that the two superpowers (and their allied 'power blocs' – shown in Source 4) did not declare war on one another, even though many people at the time feared they would. Yet many problems remained. Years of calm alternated with years of crisis, but somehow the governments of the USA and the USSR managed to maintain an uneasy balance of power. What were the reasons for this? Why wasn't there a superpower war in the 1950s and 1960s?

The reasons why

Historians have suggested six main reasons why there was not a superpower war. The following list summarises them for you, and you can find out more about them in the rest of this Unit. As you read the text and study the sources in this Unit, try to decide which you think were the most important reasons. Can you suggest any extra reasons of your own?

1. Frequent changes in superpower leadership and policy (see fact box).

2. Small-scale wars at local 'flashpoints' (see Source 4) defused the threat of all-out war – though these flashpoints led to dangers, too. (See pages 36–39 and 40–41.)

3. The superpowers fought a 'war of ideas' instead of fighting battles with tanks and bombs.

4. Superpower governments faced criticism from their own citizens (see pages 30–31).

5. Disagreements between the USSR and China over the 'correct' form of communism weakened the USSR's power and turned its attention away from the USA. This led to open conflict in 1960.

6. The superpowers' possession of deadly nuclear weapons made war more terrifying than ever before. Even worse, nuclear weapons could destroy the whole world; after a nuclear war neither superpower would survive. (See pages 28–29 and 36–39.)

Superpower Leaders and Policies 1950s–1960s

USSR

Stalin 1922–1953
The Soviet leader Joseph Stalin died in 1953, after ruling for almost 30 years. As you saw in Unit 1, his policy of Soviet expansion into Eastern Europe after the defeat of Nazi Germany in 1945 was a major factor in starting the Cold War. Stalin's motives have been debated ever since. Was his aim to defend the USSR against any future attack? Or did he aim to spread communist ideology and increase the USSR's power?

Khrushchev 1953–1964
After Stalin's death, the USSR changed. In 1953, there was a brief power-struggle between rivals plotting to succeed Stalin. The winner, Khrushchev, was a reformer who wanted to turn the USSR's economy away from heavy industry towards producing more food and a wider range of consumer goods.

Khrushchev began as a reformer in foreign policy, too. In a famous speech in 1956 he proposed a policy of co-existence, not conflict, with the capitalist world. He then went on, in a secret session, to denounce Stalin and many of Stalin's policies.

But then, after the Hungarian Uprising of 1956 (see pages 30–31), Khrushchev's foreign policy changed. It became warlike and unpredictble. He built the Berlin Wall in 1961, quarrelled with Mao Zedong, leader of communist China, caused a crisis over Soviet missile bases on Cuba, and irritated his Soviet Communist Party colleagues. They finally lost patience with him, and he was removed from power in 1964.

Brezhnev 1964–1982
After Khrushchev's downfall, the USSR's policy changed again. Khrushchev's successor, Leonid Brezhnev, aimed to avoid war between the superpowers, and helped set up the SALT (Strategic Arms Limitation Treaty) talks of 1972. This policy lasted until 1979, when the USSR decided to invade Afghanistan. You can read more about SALT and Afghanistan in Unit 4.

USA

Eisenhower and Dulles 1953–1961
In America, there were also new leaders. President Truman left office in 1953. His anti-communist policy of 'containment' was continued for a while by the next President, Dwight Eisenhower, with strong encouragment from his Secretary of State, John Foster Dulles. But Dulles died in 1959, and, after that, Eisenhower began to try and negotiate for peace with the USSR. But his policy changed suddenly after the Russians shot down an American spy plane in 1960.

Kennedy 1961–1963
John F. Kennedy became President in 1961, at a time when superpower relations were very tense. They worsened after the USA failed in its attempt to invade Cuba (the Bay of Pigs incident, 1961) and after the Cuban Missile Crisis of 1962 (see pages 36–39). Kennedy did agree to sign a Test Ban Treaty with the USSR in 1963, but, for most of his time in office, he overestimated the Soviet threat. This made him send American troops to fight against communists in Vietnam, with disastrous results in the longer term (see pages 40–41).

Johnson 1963–1969
Kennedy was assassinated in 1963. He was succeeded by Lyndon B. Johnson, who was President until 1969. His main interest was in home affairs, and he introduced a wide-ranging programme of social reforms. Overseas, he stepped up the USA's anti-communist involvement in the war in Vietnam (see pages 40–41). Many soldiers died, and the communists seemed to be winning.

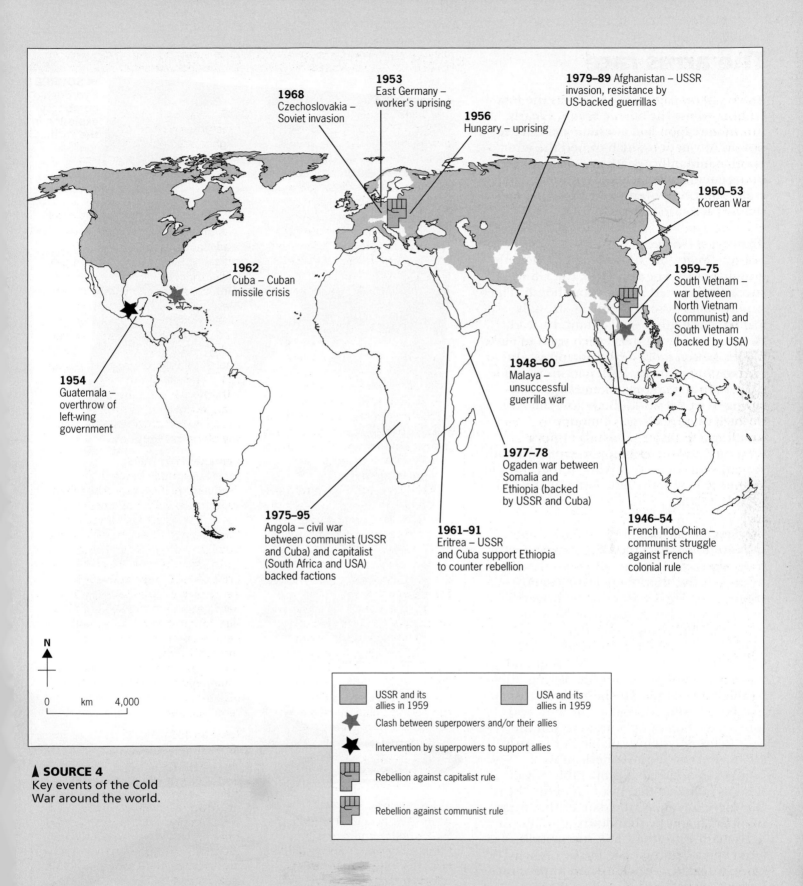

1968
Czechoslovakia –
Soviet invasion

1953
East Germany –
worker's uprising

1956
Hungary – uprising

1979–89 Afghanistan – USSR
invasion, resistance by
US-backed guerrillas

1950–53
Korean War

1962
Cuba – Cuban
missile crisis

1959–75
South Vietnam –
war between
North Vietnam
(communist) and
South Vietnam
(backed by USA)

1954
Guatemala –
overthrow of
left-wing
government

1948–60
Malaya –
unsuccessful
guerrilla war

1977–78
Ogaden war between
Somalia and
Ethiopia (backed
by USSR and Cuba)

1975–95
Angola – civil war
between communist (USSR
and Cuba) and capitalist
(South Africa and USA)
backed factions

1961–91
Eritrea – USSR
and Cuba support Ethiopia
to counter rebellion

1946–54
French Indo-China –
communist struggle
against French
colonial rule

N

0   km   4,000

USSR and its
allies in 1959

USA and its
allies in 1959

Clash between superpowers and/or their allies

Intervention by superpowers to support allies

Rebellion against capitalist rule

Rebellion against communist rule

▲ **SOURCE 4**
Key events of the Cold
War around the world.

The arms race

As we saw on page 4, the USA was the first country to use the atomic bomb. Clearly, this new weapon had awesome destructive power. Any nation which owned the atom bomb could inflict death and devastation on its enemies on an almost unimaginable scale – and could (everyone thought) use the bomb to win all wars.

The start of the race

For four years, the USA remained the only atomic power. Then, in 1949, the USSR successfully tested its own atom bomb. The superpowers were now equally strongly armed, but neither was content. Instead, they began an arms race: each tried to make bigger, better, more deadly weapons, and to amass more of them. Both nations wanted to win the arms race, and end up as the strongest in the world. Both governments devoted large amounts of money to building and testing all kinds of new weapons, and teams of top scientists in both superpowers dedicated years of their lives to inventing new, more efficient machines to deliver death.

Bombers and missiles

In November 1952, the USA tested an even more powerful nuclear weapon – the new hydrogen (or 'thermonuclear') bomb (Source 5). The USSR's first hydrogen bomb was ready the next year. Now the arms race had really speeded up. As well as building bombs and warheads, each superpower also tried to build faster and more accurate systems for 'delivering' them to an enemy target. The bomb at Hiroshima had been dropped from an aircraft, and long-range bomber planes were still the only delivery system available in the early 1950s. You can see an American B-52 bomber in Source 6. Comparable Soviet designs included the 'Bison' and the 'Bear'. But there was always the danger that these bombers might be shot down.

Then, in 1957, the USSR successfully launched a 'sputnik' satellite by rocket. The USA struggled to catch up and a space race began (see pages 34–35). Rockets would soon be used to deliver nuclear warheads and both superpowers developed ICBMs (Inter-Continental Ballistic Missiles).

◄ **SOURCE 5**
Hydrogen bomb test explosion in the Pacific.

▲ **SOURCE 6**
US nuclear strike force: a B-52 bomber.

SOURCE 7
Soviet nuclear weapons on view in Red Square, Moscow, 1966.

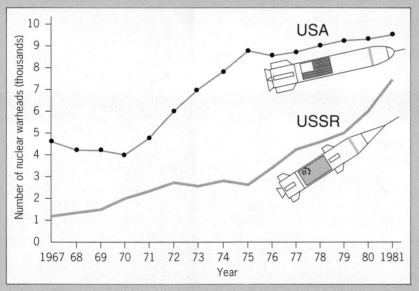

SOURCE 8
The arms race.

SOURCE 9

I know from experience that the leaders of the armed forces can be very persistent in claiming their share when it comes to allocating funds. Every commander has all sorts of convincing arguments why he should get more than anyone else. Unfortunately, there's a tendency for people who run the armed forces to be greedy and self-seeking. They're always ready to throw in your face the slogan 'if you try to economise, you'll pay in blood when war breaks out tomorrow.' I'm not denying that these men have a huge responsibility but the fact remains that the living standard of the country suffers when the budget is overloaded with allocations to unproductive branches of consumption. And today as yesterday, the most unproductive expenditures of all are those made by the armed forces.

(Khrushchev comments on the cost of the arms race.)

ICBMs

These missiles were launched from stores (called SILOS) hidden in underground bases. Sometimes these were in other countries near their target. For example, the USA had missiles based in Turkey, aimed at the USSR, and (in 1962–63) the Soviets had missiles based in Cuba, close to the USA. Because of the long distances they had to travel, these missiles were enormous – the American version was named 'Titan' (after an ancient giant). You can see some Soviet missiles in Source 7.

Although each ICBM base was well-hidden, and surrounded by armed guards, governments feared that their nuclear sites might be attacked. So, in the early 1960s, they designed missiles, like the American 'Polaris' or the Soviet SS N-5, that could be launched from moveable silos on board submarines. Once underwater, the submarines were impossible for enemy spy planes to detect. They could carry their deadly cargoes all round the world, ready to attack an enemy at its weakest point. In the late 1950s and 1960s, the USSR also built up an immensely strong navy, not only of submarines, but of surface ships as well.

MAD?

Throughout the 1950s and the 1960s, each superpower built up huge stocks of nuclear warheads. They also employed secret networks of spies to try and find out about each other's latest weapons. (You can read more about this on page 33.) Their nuclear stockpiles grew at an ever-increasing rate (Source 8). By the late 1960s, each superpower had built enough nuclear weapons to destroy the other – and the rest of the world – many times over.

This situation was known as 'MAD' – short for 'Mutually Assured Destruction'. It was supposed to make sure that neither superpower would ever attack the other – because, if it did, its own land and people would be destroyed as well.

Did 'MAD' work? In one sense, yes, because the superpowers did not fight a nuclear war. But, like the arms race itself, MAD was a very dangerous game to play – and very expensive (see Source 9).

Suppressing dissent

Stalin had ruled the USSR very toughly. Critics had been ruthlessly 'purged', along with many other people such as religious leaders, writers and scholars, whom he considered to be a danger to the state. Millions of others were condemned to a 'living death' in prisons and labour camps. This firm control continued after the Second World War.

Stalin died in 1953. After two years, Nikita Khrushchev emerged as leader. He denounced Stalin's brutal rule in a secret (but widely leaked) speech to the Communist Party Congress in 1956. He also allowed writers like Aleksandr Solzhenitsyn to publish books describing the horrors of the labour camps. People inside and outside the Soviet Union were shocked. But they also felt encouraged.

They knew that Khrushchev had freed many of Stalin's prisoners, and they believed that he was planning to allow more political debate and freedom of speech as well.

Protests

Khrushchev's criticisms of Stalin were especially welcome to people living in those Eastern European countries that Stalin had taken over at the end of the Second World War. Ever since then, they had been controlled by the USSR. All contact with the West was banned, all the media were censored, and farms and factories were ordered to produce whatever the Russians wanted. Their citizens were spied on by informers and secret police. Now, they hoped, they would have the chance to control their own lives.

CASE STUDY: HUNGARY

Before the Second World War, Hungary had a right-wing government. It was anti-Russian and anti-communist. In 1940 Hungary allied itself with Hitler. In 1944 the advancing Red Army drove the retreating Germans through Hungary. The Soviet armed forces continued to occupy Hungary after the war.

In the first elections, in 1945, the Communists only won 17% of the vote, but shared power with the victorious Peasant Party. It was a Communist Minister of Agriculture, Imre Nagy, who gave 640,000 peasants their own land, confiscated from the big landowners. This made him a hero to most Hungarians. However, as elsewhere in Eastern Europe, Hungary was soon directly under Stalin's control. One by one non-communists and even Communists who did not automatically follow Stalin, were removed. By 1948 Hungary was ruled as a one-party state by Matyas Rákosi.

Rákosi's dictatorship
• He slavishly did just what Stalin told him.
• Hungary is a rich farming country, but priority was given to industry, copying the USSR. Five-Year plans were started in 1949. Hours were long and wages low.

SOURCE 10

The peasants' and workers' sons were the most outspoken. They could ask questions like 'Isn't the delivery quota too high?' It was perhaps the peasant kids, who went home regularly and saw the misery in the villages, who were most outspoken about their situation.

(A student describes finding out about problems in agriculture.)

SOURCE 11

The Communists took over all the factories, proclaiming the slogan: 'The factory is yours – you work for yourself.' The exact opposite of this was true. They promised us everything, at the same time pulling us down into great misery.

(A factory worker describes the situation in industry.)

• Farms were collectivised, as Stalin had done in the USSR. The peasants resisted and output fell.
• Instead of recoving after the war, the standard of living fell by 5% between 1949 and 1955.

◄ **SOURCE 12**
Hungarians burning pictures of Stalin in the street, 1956.

SOURCE 13

"I've seen officers of the AVH that were captured strung up on the trees outside and people started kicking them saying: 'That's for torturing my father', 'That's for torturing my brother.' I would imagine they all got kicked to death and all of a sudden thousands of forints [Hungarian money] appeared in notes and they were stuffing the money into the AVOs' mouths and pockets. . . . It was a way of saying 'You were a paid torturer, so here's your final payment.'

(A Hungarian who later escaped to the West describes how people took revenge on the hated 'AVOs'.)"

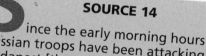

SOURCE 14

Since the early morning hours Russian troops have been attacking Budapest [the capital of Hungary] and our people. Please tell the world of the treacherous attack against our struggle for liberty. Help! Help! Help!

(One of the last broadcasts from a radio station held by Hungarian rebels.)

▼ **SOURCE 15**
Soviet officer shouting at a Western cameraman, Hungary, 1956.

The Rising

The people grumbled (Sources 10 and 11), but were afraid to act. Rákosi set up a secret police force of 100,000 – the AVH (AVOs). There were police informers everywhere; 200,000 people were arrested and put in prison.

Khrushchev's speech about Stalin in 1956 led to protests in Hungary. First, Rákosi was forced to resign, then Nagy became Prime Minister. He appealed for calm, but the people on the streets wanted revenge for years of repression (Source 12). Statues of Stalin were sent crashing to the ground. The hated AVOs were sought out and lynched (Source 13). There were calls for free elections with other parties.

Nagy declared that Hungary wanted to be a NEUTRAL country and was leaving the Warsaw Pact. He took the Western nations' talk of 'freeing countries from communism' seriously and called on the UN for support.

This was too much for Khrushchev. He sent 1,000 tanks into Budapest to crush the rising (Source 14). Three thousand people were killed. Nagy was arrested and later executed. The Western nations did nothing. The Hungarians' desperate calls for help (Source 15) were not answered.

Assessment

1 • *Traditional dislike of the USSR*
   • *Bad working conditions*
   • *Forced collectivisation of peasant farms*
   • *AVH terror*
   • *Lack of freedom*
   • *Fall in standard of living*
   Choose three of the above items and explain why they helped to cause the 1956 Hungarian Rising.

2 *Show how your three choices can be linked together.*

3 *Why did the Hungarian Rising take place when it did and not years earlier or later?*

4 *Why did the Western nations not answer the Hungarians' calls for help?*

Keeping control

◄ **SOURCE 16**
The Berlin Wall being built, 1961.

▼ **SOURCE 17**
A Russian tank in the centre of Prague, the Czech capital, surrounded by angry students, 1968.

The Berlin Wall, 1961

After Hungary, other Eastern European nations did not dare to challenge Soviet power. But many individual citizens tried to escape by fleeing to the West. The divided city of Berlin was a favourite refuge. By 1961, 2 million people from East Germany had found freedom there. Once again, Khrushchev felt threatened. He ordered a massive concrete wall to be built along the border between the communist and capitalist zones of the city (Source 16). It was manned by armed guards who had orders to shoot and kill anyone who tried to cross it illegally.

Czechoslovakia, 1968

There was another attempt to break free of Soviet control, in Czechoslovakia in the late 1960s. This time it was fuelled by economic as well as political grievances. Before 1948 Czechoslovakia had been a prosperous state, with a proud cultural heritage and well-developed industry. But years of communist government by leaders loyal to Moscow had damaged all that. In 1967 a leading Czech economist, Otto Sik, suggested that a free economy would bring greater prosperity. It would lead to greater political freedom, too. Sik's ideas were welcomed by many people, including Alexander Dubcek, who became leader of the Czech Communist Party in 1968. He introduced a programme of social and economic reforms which he called 'Communism with a human face'.

Dubcek's reforming policies were very popular in Czechoslovakia, but once again alarmed the Soviet leadership. Brezhnev demanded that Dubcek resign. When he refused, the Soviet army was sent in to crush the 'revolt' (Source 17).

Suppressing dissent – in the Americas

Just as the USSR expected the states of Eastern Europe to stay loyal, so the USA expected the states of Central and South America and the Caribbean not to join the communists. In fact, in some cases, the USA suppressed rebels who were not communists at all, but were merely rebelling against right-wing governments. Here are just four examples:

• In 1954 the USA backed soldiers who overthrew the left-wing government of Guatemala, which was planning to NATIONALISE the large US-owned banana plantations.

• In 1961 the USA backed an invasion of Cuba at the Bay of Pigs intended to overthrow the left-wing government of Fidel Castro (see page 36).

• In 1965 a rebellion in the Dominican Republic against the right-wing government was crushed by 23,000 US soldiers.

• In 1970 Salvador Allende, a socialist, was elected President of Chile (see Source 18). The USA retaliated by undermining Chile's economy. In 1973 Allende was overthrown by soldiers secretly backed by the US government. Brutal military rule was imposed under General Pinochet.

With the exception of Cuba, the USSR did not interfere in any of these actions. Just as in the case of Hungary, the superpowers were ready to let each other do what they liked in 'their own backyards'.

▲ **SOURCE 18**
Salvador Allende, socialist President of Chile.

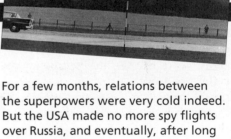

Spies and spying

During the Cold War, each superpower maintained a worldwide network of spies. Their job was to try and find out about the other side's resources, policies and plans. Spies also bought information from informers.

Spies and spying were so important during the Cold War that they became part of popular culture. Novels, films and TV plays about spying all achieved great success. In them, spies were often portrayed as glamorous heroes, like James Bond (created by Ian Fleming), whose adventures featured an entertaining, escapist, combination of exotic locations, sex and the latest technological wizardry.

But, in fact, being a spy was a risky, and sometimes rather sordid occupation. It could involve skill, courage, quick-thinking and dedication, but also murder, blackmail and deception.

Spying was also a very serious crime. Many people were shocked when, as early as 1953, the US government executed Julius and Ethel Rosenburg for passing American secrets to the USSR, but, during the Cold War, both superpowers took a hard line.

The U-2 incident

In the early 1960s, before accurate ground-to-air missiles had been developed, the USA used special spy-planes to fly over enemy land. These were equipped with cameras to photograph airfields, weapons silos, and other military bases, and were designed to fly so high that Russian fighter jets could not reach them (see photograph).

But spy-planes did not always manage to stay out of enemy reach. In May 1960, an American U-2 spy plane flying over Russia was shot down by Russian jets. Gary Powers, the pilot, was taken prisoner.

The 'U-2 incident', as this came to be known, caused a period of serious tension between the USA and USSR. The Russians demanded an apology, but US President Eisenhower refused to give one. In retaliation, Soviet leader Khrushchev refused to continue a high-level 'summit' meeting that had been arranged to discuss peace.

For a few months, relations between the superpowers were very cold indeed. But the USA made no more spy flights over Russia, and eventually, after long negotiations, Gary Powers was returned to the USA in February 1962 in exchange for a Soviet spy.

JAMES BOND IS BACK!

his new incredible women!
his new incredible enemies!
his new incredible adventures!

HARRY SALTZMAN AND ALBERT R. BROCCOLI PRESENT IAN FLEMING'S **FROM RUSSIA WITH LOVE**

How did the Cold War affect the space race?

In 1961, President John F. Kennedy of the USA made a rousing speech. In it he declared his country's aim of putting a person on the Moon by the end of the decade (see Source 19). The speech was a call to action for all American space scientists, and a signal that the American government was willing to invest enormous sums of money in space research.

But Kennedy's speech signalled much more than that. It was a proud boast and a challenge. Kennedy was declaring his faith in his country's scientific expertise and challenging the only other nation with similar skills and resources – that is, the USSR – to equal the USA, or do better.

Scientific progress or political prestige?
Kennedy's speech was just the latest and most dramatic instalment in a long-running contest between the two superpowers. Both wanted to demonstrate that their technological achievements – and therefore their government and society – were the best. There was great heroism among astronauts from both nations, and some scientific progress too – such as discoveries in materials science and in AERONAUTICAL engineering. But the space race was above all else a matter of political prestige.

As you can see from the first few entries in the time chart below, both superpowers could lay claim to be continuing traditions established by important early 20th-century scientific pioneers.

The 1960s space programme was only possible because of rocket technology

SOURCE 19

I believe that this nation should commit itself to achieving the goal, before the decade is out, of landing a man on the Moon.

(US President John F. Kennedy, 1961.)

Time chart

Advances in the space race

1903 Konstantin Tsiolokovsky (Russia) develops ideas for space rockets fuelled by liquid gas.
1923 Herman Oberth (Germany) publishes *The Rocket and Interplanetary Space*.
1926 Robert Goddard (USA) develops first liquid-fuelled rocket.
1942 Werner von Braun (Germany) designs V2 rocket. At the end of Second World War he goes to work in USA.
1957 USSR launches first satellite – Sputnik 1.
1961 (April) Yuri Gagarin (USSR) becomes first man in space. Makes full orbit of Earth.
1961 (May) First American man in space, but not a full orbit.
1962 John Glenn (USA): first American space orbit.
1962 Mariner 2 (USA): first successful interplanetary probe, sent towards Venus.
1965 Alexei Leonov (USSR) makes first space walk.
1969 Neil Armstrong and Buzz Aldrin (USA): first men on the Moon.
1972 American Moon landing programme ends.
1973 Skylab (USA): first orbiting space station.
1977 Voyager 2 (USA) sent on one-way trip to collect information about Jupiter and send photographs back to Earth.
1981 Start of space shuttle programme (USA): re-usable craft taking passengers and cargo into space.
1988 Russian cosmonaut stays in space for 365 days – a new record.
1990s Plans for joint USA–USSR space missions.

◄ **SOURCE 20**
A model of Sputnik 1.

▲ **SOURCE 21**
A rocket launch for another space flight during the 1960s. This one is a US Gemini mission, 6 April 1966.

developed by German scientists during the Second World War. Before Braun invented the V2 rocket (see time chart), no flying machines had generated enough energy to blast free from the Earth's gravitational field.

Who won the space race?

Kennedy made his speech in 1961. At that time, the USSR seemed to be winning the space race, and the Americans were beginning to feel shamefaced. If their country was rich, powerful and prosperous as they claimed, why were they getting left behind? Russia made the first great breakthrough in space, with the flight of Sputnik 1 (Source 20). The next major advance was human space flight (Source 22), also made by the USSR, although the USA was able to launch its first manned space flight only three weeks later.

Kennedy died in 1963. Even so, the pace of the superpower space race did not slacken. Space 'firsts' came thick and fast. The Americans and Russians made more and more space flights (see Source 21), although gradually they came to aim at different goals.

The USA did succeed, just, in fulfilling Kennedy's dream. The first men landed on the Moon in July 1969. After that, the USA and USSR concentrated on building space stations that can stay on orbit around the Earth, and in developing probes to send back information about neighbouring planets and stars.

Co-operation in space

The Russians have also undertaken medical research into the effects of long periods spent in space, while the Americans have built the space shuttle, re-usable for short flights into space. Scientists from many nations now take part in space programmes, and information is published and shared.

Space research is so expensive that no one nation has the political will or the money to undertake vast projects on its own. Increasingly, co-operation has replaced competition as nations realise that the space race is far too expensive for any one country to continue on its own.

The space race is at an end.

▲ **SOURCE 22**
Yuri Gagarin, the Russian cosmonaut who was the first person to orbit the Earth, at a height of over 300 km on 12 April 1961.

Assessment

1 Use the timechart to describe what the space race was like.

2 Why did space exploration become part of the Cold War?

3 Who won the space race?

The Cuban Missile Crisis, 1962

The cartoon (Source 23) shows the Cuban Missile Crisis of October 1962 as an old-fashioned western gunfight between Kennedy and Khrushchev (with Castro as Khrushchev's sidekick).

In fact it was not a joke. The weapons involved were not six-shooters but nuclear missiles capable of killing millions of people. It was the moment when the Cold War came closest to being a real war.

Cuba is an island in the Caribbean, only 145 kilometres from the American coast. For many years, American businesses had owned property in Cuba, and Cuban rulers had been friendly towards the US government. But in 1959, the Cuban government was overthrown in a revolution, led by Fidel Castro (Source 24).

The Bay of Pigs Incident

Castro's followers were mostly liberals, but included some communists. Their policies were mainly NATIONALIST: they wanted Cuba to be free of foreign influence. This included the USA. Castro took over all the American-owned land in Cuba, and nationalised American businesses too. When angry Americans refused to trade with him, Castro sold Cuba's sugar crop (its main export) to the USSR, instead.

In the 1960 presidential campaign, Kennedy had spoken of a 'missile gap'. He claimed that the USSR had more powerful rockets. As a new, young, liberal President, he had to appear tough in opposing communism (see Source 26). The Castro revolution seemed to have given the USSR an ally right on the USA's doorstep. In 1961, therefore, Kennedy backed a group of anti-communist Cubans, living in the USA, who were planning a rebellion against Castro's rule. With American help, the Cuban rebels launched an invasion. They tried to land at the Bay of Pigs, on the south coast of Cuba, but were driven back by Castro's troops.

This 'incident' did nothing to improve relations between Cuba and the USA – but it did encourage Cuba and the USSR to become even closer friends. Castro came more under the influence of communists. It was a blow to Kennedy's prestige.

▲ **SOURCE 23**
A cartoon of 1962 showing US President Kennedy, on the left, and, on the right, Fidel Castro on a donkey with Soviet leader Khrushchev behind him.

▼ **SOURCE 24**
Fidel Castro. In 1959, after two earlier attempts had failed, he successfully overthrew the US-backed dictatorship of Batista.

A base for missiles

The Soviet government, led by Khrushchev, was naturally pleased to welcome a new communist nation as an ally. But communist Cuba meant more to the USSR than that. There was, in fact, no 'missile gap'. If anything, the USA was in the stronger position. Khrushchev realised that Cuba would be an ideal site to build a missile base. At this time, 1962, the USSR had not yet developed 'travelling' missiles that could be fired from submarines. Weapons launched from Cuba would take only 17 minutes to reach anywhere (except Alaska) in the USA, and, if aimed at big cities, they would kill at least 80 million people (see Source 25). Soviet bases in Cuba would provide a good 'balance', Khrushchev thought, for the American missile bases close to the Soviet border with Turkey.

In 1962, American intelligence agents suspected that Soviet missiles were being sent to Cuba by ship. But it took time to get proof. By 16 October, they had it. They showed US President Kennedy photographs of Soviet missile bases (like the one in Source 27 on page 38) being built in Cuba. What should Kennedy do?

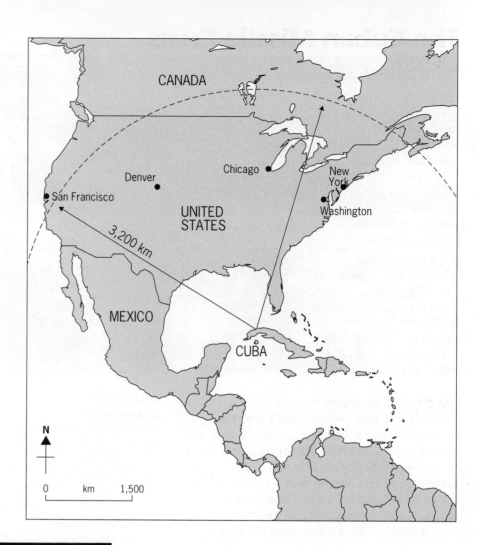

△ SOURCE 25
Map showing how missiles based in Cuba could have hit most of the major cities in the USA.

What should Kennedy do?

	Option	Result
A	Do nothing.	Kennedy would look weak.
B	Air strike on Cuba with non-nuclear weapons.	Sites could be destroyed, but Soviet workers might be killed. Danger of escalation to world war.
C	Invade Cuba.	Heavy US casualties. Danger of escalation to world war.
D	Blockade Cuba so the missiles cannot be put in place.	Confrontation with USSR but no loss of life.
E	Nuclear attack on Cuba.	Strong danger of nuclear war.

1. Which of these options would you choose, and why?

2. Which do you think Kennedy chose?

SOURCE 26

Let every nation know, whether it wishes us well or ill, that we shall pay any price, bear any burden, meet any hardship, support any friend, oppose any foe, in order to assure the survival and success of liberty.

(An extract from the speech made by Kennedy when he became President, January 1961)

The Cuban Missile Crisis

MISSILE ERECTOR

5 TRUCKS UNDER CAMOUFLAGE NETTING

CABLE

THEODOLITE STATION

5 TRUCKS UNDER CAMOUFLAGE NETTING

MISSILE SHELTER TENTS

On 22 October 1962, President Kennedy declared a naval blockade of Cuba (see Source 28). The Soviet cargo ships with the missiles on board were heading for Cuba. What would happen? The world was fearful (see Source 29). Was this the head-on clash between the superpowers which people had been expecting ever since the Cold War began? Would there be a nuclear war? Khrushchev thought that because Kennedy was young, he was inexperienced (Kennedy was 45, Khrushchev was 67). He thought Kennedy was weak because the USA had taken no action over the building of the Berlin Wall in 1961 (see page 32). Now Kennedy had pushed the situation to a real confrontation.

Khrushchev ordered his ships to turn back. The world breathed a sigh of relief.

But that was not the end of the crisis. What about the missile sites in Cuba? On 26 October Kennedy received a message from Khrushchev offering to think about dismantling the sites if the US blockade was lifted (see Source 31). Kennedy was just thinking about how to react to this when another message arrived the next day (see Source 31). This seemed to link Soviet withdrawal to the bigger issue of US bases in Turkey as well.

Now what should Kennedy do? In Source 30, Robert Kennedy, the President's brother, describes the mood in the

▲ **SOURCE 27**
Photograph taken by a US spy plane over Cuba, 1962. The parts of the base have been labelled.

▼ **SOURCE 28**
A Soviet cargo ship with the missiles in crates in the deck.

L. KOMSOMOL WITH MISSILES UNCOVERED (9 NOVEMBER)

President's office in the White House. Robert Kennedy suggested replying to Khrushchev's first message only. His brother agreed. He told Khrushchev that if Soviet missiles were removed from Cuba the US blockade would end and there would be no US invasion of the island. If Kennedy did not have a reply by 29 October, US forces would invade Cuba. Again war seemed imminent. Then, on 28 October, Khrushchev replied, accepting Kennedy's offer. The Cuban Missile Crisis was over.

SOURCE 29

We really did think that the world was going to end. I was a schoolchild in 1962. I think I first realised how serious the situation was when, at morning assembly, our headmistress – an immensely dignified older woman – actually got down on her knees in front of the whole school and said urgent prayers, begging God for peace. We children had to kneel to say our prayers every day, but she had never done anything like this before. We were frightened and impressed. We were all very scared at the thought of a nuclear war.

(Remembered by a British school student aged 12 in 1962.)

SOURCE 30

There was a feeling that the noose was tightening. What was going to happen in Berlin, in Turkey, if we attacked Cuba? We were deciding really for all mankind . . . there were arguments, sharp disagreements. Everyone was tense, some were near exhaustion – all were weighed down with worry.

(President Kennedy's brother Robert describes the mood in the White House during the crisis.)

SOURCE 31

A

If assurances were given that the United States would not attack Cuba, and the blockade was lifted, the question of the missile sites in Cuba would be entirely different. We and you ought not to pull on the ends of the rope in which you have tied the knot of war, because the more the two of us pull, the tighter that knot will be tied.

B

You are worried by Cuba . . . because it is 90 miles from America, but Turkey is next to us. Our sentries walk up and down and look at each other. I therefore make this proposal. We agree to remove from Cuba those means which you regard as offensive. The United States will for its part remove its means from Turkey.

(Extracts from letters sent by Khrushchev to Kennedy on (A) 26 October and (B) 27 October 1962.)

What should Khrushchev do?

Options

A   Order his ships to turn round.

B   Order his ships to go on.

C   Order his ships to stop.

D   Negotiate a deal with Kennedy.

E   Cause a distraction – invade West Berlin.

F   Send Soviet warships to support his cargo ships.

1. What do you think would be the results of each of these options?

2. Which would you choose?

3. Which do you think Khrushchev chose?

Assessment

1   *Look at the 'Options' boxes on pages 37 and 39. Which options did Kennedy and Khrushchev in fact choose?*

2   *What do you think were their motives, in each case?*

3   *Many people in the USA claimed that the USA had 'won' the Cuban Missile Crisis. Do you agree with this claim?*

4   *Khrushchev came in for a lot of criticism in the USSR for his actions. Did he deserve this criticism?*

The superpowers felt that the crisis had taught them some lessons:
• That they had a tremendous responsibility for the peace of the whole world.
• That they should keep in closer contact. In 1963 a 'hotline' between the White House and the Kremlin was set up.
• Nuclear arms talks should begin. In 1963 a test-ban treaty was signed.

Why was the USA fighting in Vietnam?

The Vietnam War began as a struggle by ordinary Vietnamese people for freedom from foreign rule. First, they fought against Japanese soldiers, who had invaded Vietnam during the Second World War. Next, they fought against the government of France, which had ruled Vietnam as a colony for many years (see time chart).

The freedom-fighters in Vietnam were led by Ho Chi Minh. He was a communist, and most of his followers were communists, too. They fought bravely, and many ordinary Vietnamese people admired them. They supported them – even if they did not really agree with communist ideology – because it was the best way of helping to drive foreigners from their land.

In its early stages, the war in Vietnam had nothing to do with the USA. So how did the USA get involved? America and France were allies. France was fighting to retain its colonial power against Ho Chi Minh and his communists (now backed by communist China). The French government asked America for help. The Americans agreed. They disapproved of French colonialism, but feared communism more.

The 'Domino Theory'

The Americans had another reason for getting involved in Vietnam. They believed in the 'domino theory'. They thought the governments of South-East Asia (South Vietnam, Cambodia, Laos, Thailand, Burma and India) were unsteadily balanced between communism and capitalism, like a set of dominoes balanced on one edge. They feared that if South Vietnam – the first 'domino' – toppled over into communism, then all the other countries would overbalance and become communist, too. This would create a third superpower BLOC, centred on communist China, which might ally with the USSR. Together they could defeat America.

The war gets worse

After 1954, when French rule ended, Vietnam was divided into two rival states with different ideologies – communist North Vietnam and capitalist South Vietnam (Source 32). The rivals soon became outright enemies. Ho Chi Minh encouraged communist guerrilla fighters (called the 'Vietcong') to attack the government of the South. The Vietcong were very successful. To try and defeat them, the American government sent helicopter gunships, landmines and bombs. By 1964, US planes were averaging 164 bombing raids a day. By 1969, there were over half a million American troops (Source 34) fighting the Vietcong in South Vietnam.

▲ **SOURCE 32**
Vietnam and its neighbours:
the 'Domino Theory'.

SOURCE 33 ►
Many ordinary Vietnamese were victims of the fighting and, like this family, forced to leave their homes.

▲ **SOURCE 34**
US troops in action in the jungles of Vietnam, 1967.

The war devastated a fertile and very beautiful land. It killed around 2 million soldiers (from both sides), plus an unknown number of Vietnamese civilians. The Americans used weapons such as napalm (a burning mixture which sticks to human flesh) to destroy villages and farms, and poisonous chemicals, such as 'Agent Orange', to remove the lush green leaves from rainforests where the Vietcong were hiding. These tactics caused outrage worldwide, but continued until 1969.

By 1969, the USA realised that it could not win. Over 50,000 US troops had been killed in action, and over 150,000 had been injured. American deaths were now averaging 300 per week, but the Vietcong seemed as strong as ever. There were anti-war riots and protests at home. So peace talks began, and US President Nixon (elected 1968) started to 'bring the boys home'. A formal peace treaty was agreed in 1973, but, within two years, troops from North Vietnam had invaded and conquered the south.

Hearts and minds

The Americans lost the war. Why?
• The government of South Vietnam (which the USA supported) was inefficient, and, some said, corrupt. It was not trusted by many Vietnamese people. They did not support it with their hearts or their minds.
• Although the Vietcong often fought brutally, the communists were still respected.
• The Vietcong were experienced, committed and dedicated; they had already been successful against two foreign powers: Japan and France.
• The Vietcong used guerrilla tactics – sudden ambushes, bombs and raids; they had secret jungle hide-outs; they fought by night. They were almost impossible to defeat.
• American soldiers found fighting in Vietnam very scary: they were far from home, in hot, unhealthy jungles, and in constant danger of attack. They had no way of knowing which Vietnamese people were friendly, and which supported the Vietcong.
• As the war became increasingly brutal, many American soldiers were appalled by all the suffering they saw – among their comrades and among the Vietnamese.

Time chart

War in Vietnam

1943–45 Ho Chi Minh, leader of the Vietnamese communists, fights against Japanese invaders.
1945 War against Japan ends; French refuse independence. Ho Chi Minh starts war against French colonial rulers.
1954 Rebels defeat French at Dien Bien Phu. French colonial rulers leave.
1954–55 Indo-China is divided into four parts: North and South Vietnam, Cambodia and Laos. Ho Chi Minh becomes ruler of communist North Vietnam; rulers opposed to communists and friendly with USA lead South Vietnam; Cambodia and Laos become independent states.
1956 Democratic elections in South Vietnam cancelled by anti-communist government; communist rebels – called the Vietcong – begin to fight against government.
USA sends army advisers, but Vietcong become increasingly powerful.
1964 All known communists in South Vietnam and their Buddhist supporters imprisoned without trial. US Congress grants US President Johnson powers to take military action.
1965 125,000 American troops land in South Vietnam to support South Vietnam government. US planes bomb North Vietnam.
1967 American troops in South Vietnam now total over half a million. They are joined by soldiers from America's Cold War allies: South Korea, Australia, New Zealand and Thailand. Widespread protests in America and Europe against American action in Vietnam.
1968 Tet Offensive. Attack by Vietcong plus communist troops from North Vietnam is driven back, but thousands of American soldiers killed and injured. US President Johnson begins to think America cannot win the Vietnam War.
At home in USA, American public shocked by scale of killing, and by daily TV pictures of war. Anti-war protests increase.
Peace talks between North and South Vietnam begin in Paris.
1968 Fighting spreads to Cambodia and Laos. US planes bomb Cambodia.
1969 President Johnson retires. New US President Nixon starts to withdraw US troops from Vietnam.
1971–72 Fighting continues. American public opinion increasingly against the war.
1973 Ceasefire agreed between North and South Vietnam. Last American troops leave Vietnam.
1974 Peace talks collapse; war begins again.
1975 North Vietnam invades and conquers South Vietnam.

• People at home in the USA were also shocked by the deaths and the violence – especially when it began to reported every night on their TV screens. Soldiers' families never knew, when they watched the TV news, whether they would see their own sons and brothers being blown up by a Vietcong bomb. Massive protests called for an end to the war and forced President Johnson not to seek re-election in 1968.

Change or continuity?

In this Unit, we will look at the 'second phase' of the Cold War, in the 1970s and early 1980s. We will see how both superpowers sought to find ways of continuing their struggle for supremacy without engaging in face-to-face war.

We will also see how governments and people in both superpowers began to count the costs – in economic and human terms – of armies, weapons, and strict government control. After almost 30 years, what effect was the Cold War having on each superpower's society at home?

Key Questions

How did superpower relations change during the 1970s and early 1980s?

How did the superpowers try to win power through non-military means?

Was the cost of new weapons becoming too expensive?

What were the social and political costs of the Cold War?

The years 1970–1984 were a time of contrasts. Some events, such as US President Nixon's friendly visits to Moscow and Communist China (Source 1), seemed to relax tensions between the superpowers. Other changes, like the American 'Star Wars' programme planned by US President Reagan (Source 2), seemed to revive old hostilities.

Ideological war
But there were similarities, as well as contrasts, between the two superpowers. Both continued to attack their rival in public – proclaiming the USA's capitalism or the USSR's communism to be 'bad' and 'wrong' (Source 3). Both declared that history was on their side, and that they were, eventually, bound to win. They probably both believed this.

Both superpowers looked for, and found, ways of opposing one another without actually fighting a war. They won support throughout the world by sending aid to friendly or

SOURCE 1
'Ping Pong diplomacy', 1971. The improvement in relations between the USA and Communist China after President Nixon's visit to China was emphasised by events such as this friendly sporting contest between the two nations.

SOURCE 2
Ronald Reagan.

SOURCE 3

'An evil empire . . . the focus of evil in the modern world.'

'I believe that communism is another sad, bizarre chapter in human history whose last pages even now are being written.'

(Ronald Reagan, March 1983.)

The Reagan administration has 'dangerous, inhuman policies'. . . . It is 'pushing mankind to the brink of disaster'.

'Certainly, we take the view that the capitalist order will be replaced by the socialist order . . . we believe this in the way people believe the sun will rise tomorrow morning.'

(Yuri Andropov, 1984.)

client states, and by supporting civil wars, protests and rebellions inside their rival's 'client states'.

Costs and consequences
At the same time, however, both superpowers were coming to realise that enormously expensive military spending was not necessarily a good thing for their people at home. The costs of the arms race were spiralling higher and higher. Both nations also had to face up to the fact that a full-scale nuclear war was likely to result in the destruction of all civilisation on Earth – including their own.

For all these reasons – personal contacts by leaders, wars of words, 'substitute' conflicts, worries about financial and social costs, and the fear of total ANNIHILATION – the superpowers managed to survive the period 1970–1984 in a state of uneasy peace. In the rest of this Unit, you will see how this was achieved.

Two steps forward, one step back?

US President Nixon began to withdraw American troops from Vietnam in 1969. Although that did not immediately end the fighting there (see pages 40–41), it seemed like the beginning of peace. By the early 1970s, the Vietnamese peace seemed to be 'spilling over' into other areas of superpower relations, as leaders of both the USA and the USSR began a policy of détente. You can see from the time chart how they put this policy into practice. Their greatest achievement was the SALT 1 agreement, which aimed to limit future nuclear weapons.

SALT 1 did not mean that either superpower got rid of its existing weapons. Both sides already possessed sufficient firepower to destroy the world several times over. And both sides still tried to outsmart the other. Because SALT limited the total number of weapons that either superpower could own, they both designed new MIRV missiles. Each MIRV only counted as one weapon in the SALT reckoning, but it could deliver many separate, individually targeted warheads.

That was hardly 'fair play'. But SALT 1 was a beginning. There were further advances, too, such as the Helsinki Agreement of 1975, which finally recognised the post-1945 boundaries of Europe (for long a cause for quarrels between the USA and the USSR). For the first time ever, Russian and American scientists worked on a combined programme of space research.

Personalities and priorities

The personalities and political priorities of individual superpower leaders were also important (Source 4). Some leaders aimed at détente for its own sake. After watching years of anti-war protests directed against US governments, President Carter (who was motivated by his Christian faith) and President Nixon (a very able negotiator) welcomed the popularity they won as peace-makers. Others, like Soviet leader Brezhnev, had different political priorities. Brezhnev welcomed détente because he recognised the immense perils of all-out nuclear war, but also because peace with

▲ **SOURCE 4**
US President Nixon and Soviet leader Brezhnev during Nixon's visit to Moscow, 1974.

USA TODAY/International Edition · TUESDAY, NOVEMBER 19, 1985 · 5

Advertisement

THANK YOU, MR. PRESIDENT, FOR HOLDING FAST ON YOUR HISTORIC STRATEGIC DEFENSE INITIATIVE, THE HIGH ROAD TO PEACE IN THE WORLD!

▲ **SOURCE 5**
Part of a US newspaper advertisement supporting the Strategic Defense Initiative (SDI), commonly known as 'Star Wars'. Satellites in space would destroy incoming Soviet missiles using lasers.

America left him free to concentrate on suppressing dangerous dissent in the USSR and its satellite states.

Setbacks

However, this 'Brezhnev Doctrine' led to a serious setback in the process of détente in 1979. The US Congress refused to ratify the SALT 2 treaty to demonstrate its anger over the USSR's invasion of Afghanistan in 1979. Détente received a further blow when Ronald Reagan was elected President of the USA in 1980. An avowed anti-communist, though personally friendly and peace-loving, Reagan caused confusion and some anxiety among international diplomats. The situation worsened in 1984 when the USA decided to invest in a new range of 'Star Wars' weapons, to be based in space (Source 5).

Time chart

Key moments in USA–USSR relations, 1969–1984

1969 SALT (Strategic Arms Limitation Treaty) talks start in Vienna between USA and USSR.

1970 First successful test launch of Poseidon underwater missile by USA.

1970 USA now has MIRV missiles – each with multiple, independently targeted warheads.

1971 'Ping-Pong diplomacy' – US and Chinese table tennis players take part in tournament. This is the first meeting between the USA and Communist China for 22 years. The USA does not want China and the USSR to make an alliance. Together, they would be stronger than the USA.

1971 Communist China becomes a member of the United Nations.

1971 USA–USSR Nuclear Accidents Notification Agreement – to avoid accidental nuclear attacks.

1972 US President Nixon visits China, and meets Mao Zedong.

1972 The first Strategic Arms Limitation Treaty (SALT 1) is signed between USA and USSR. Both sides agree to end the manufacture of nuclear weapons.

1973 US President Nixon visits Moscow, and meets General Secretary Brezhnev.

1973 Mutual and Balanced Forces talks between NATO and Warsaw Pact nations begin in Vienna.

1974 USA–USSR Threshold Test Ban Treaty limits the number of underground nuclear tests.

1975 Helsinki Agreement – US President Carter and USSR leader Brezhnev agree to recognise existing borders in Europe. (The Helsinki Agreement also laid down international standards for human rights.)

1975 Russian and American astronauts in joint space mission.

1977 USA tests extra-deadly 'neutron bomb'.

1978 US President Carter announces that he will postpone decision over production of neutron bomb.

1979 Soviet troops invade Afghanistan, a former Soviet 'client state', where there had been political upheaval.

1979 SALT 2 agreement, limiting the number of strategic offensive weapons, is signed. But USA refuses to ratify (confirm) it, to show its disapproval of Soviet invasion of Afghanistan.

1979 NATO plans to modernise its nuclear weapons by siting 464 ground-launched Cruise missiles and 108 Pershing II medium range missiles in Europe.

1980 USA and its allies boycott Moscow Olympic Games.

1980 President Reagan elected in USA; his policy is to take a firm stand against USSR. New arms race begins: US defence expenditure increased.

1981 USA announces plans to build new 'stealth' bomber, virtually undetectable by USSR radar.

1982 US President Reagan's 'evil empire' speech (see Source 3 on page 43).

1984 USA–USSR agreement to improve the operation of the 'hot line' – the private telephone line between government leaders, to be used if nuclear war threatened.

1984 USA announces Strategic Defense Initiative ('Star Wars') – a range of weapons in space designed to destroy ICBMs (Inter-Continental Ballistic Missiles) approaching from the USSR before they reached the USA.

1984 START (Strategic Arms Reduction Treaty) talks begin between USA and USSR, but make little progress, because of USA's Star Wars policy.

1984 Cruise missiles arrive in Europe (see 1979 above).

1984 Soviet diplomats walk out of START talks in Geneva in protest at Cruise missiles.

Superpower leaders, 1970–1985

USA
Richard M. Nixon 1969–1974
Gerald R. Ford 1974–1977
Jimmy Carter 1977–1981
Ronald W. Reagan 1981–1989

USSR
Alexei N. Kosygin 1964–1966 (shared power with Brezhnev)
Leonid I. Brezhnev 1964–1982
Yuri V. Andropov 1983–1984
Konstantin U. Chernenko 1984–1985

Investigation

Détente is a French word meaning 'relaxation', or 'easing of tension'. In terms of relations between the superpowers from 1970 to 1984 it could mean anything from friendly games of table tennis to binding agreements to limit nuclear weapons.

• Look at the time chart on this page, and find four different examples of the process of détente during the period 1970 to 1984.

• Explain how each of them helped to relax the tension between the USA and the USSR.

• What were the motives of each superpower that lay behind each one?

• Make two lists: (1) Years when détente was making good progress. (2) Years when détente was going badly.

How did détente happen? It could be encouraged (or harmed) by individual politicians, particular policies or certain events.

Look at the evidence on these pages about individual leaders of the USA and USSR and their policies. Explain what influence (positive or negative) three of them had on the process of détente.

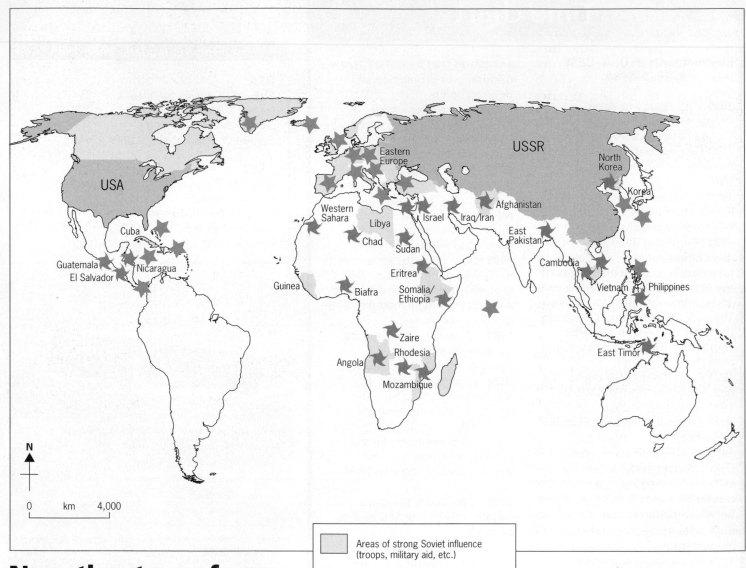

Areas of strong Soviet influence (troops, military aid, etc.)

Members of NATO

Major wars/guerrilla conflicts

Major US overseas bases

▲ **SOURCE 6**
US and Soviet bases, spheres of influence, and major conflicts.

New theatres of war

Although there was détente between the superpowers during the period 1970 to 1984, the world was not at peace. To take just one year as an example: in 1983, out of the 164 nations in the world, 45 were actively fighting in 40 different wars (Source 6). And, although Russian and American troops were not fighting face to face, the superpowers were deeply involved in many of these conflicts. In 1983, the USA was supplying weapons to 20 of the nations at war, and the USSR was supplying weapons to 13. At around the same time, the USA and the USSR, which together contained about 11 per cent of the world's population, had 23 per cent of the world's armed forces, accounted for 60 per cent of the world's total expenditure on weapons and 80 per cent of all spending on new weapons research, and owned 97 per cent of nuclear weapons in the world.

Friendship and help
The superpowers were also sending advisers and technical experts (Source 7) to the nations at war, and to many more of their allies and friends. Some of these experts were military specialists. Others, like America's famous 'Peace Corps', aimed to 'win friends and influence people' through

▲ SOURCE 7
Members of the Sandinista (FSLN) army in Nicaragua, with Soviet-supplied AK47 rifles.

peaceful means, such as building roads and hospitals, improving electricity and water supplies, and offering advice to farmers. On the whole, the Soviet Union proved more successful than the USA at this 'friendship war' (Source 8), but the Americans also took it very seriously indeed.

Bases overseas

Weapons stockpiles continued to grow, despite SALT 1 and 2, and technology became increasingly sophisticated. In 1983, the USSR possessed 8,000 nuclear missiles capable of reaching the American mainland; the Americans had 10,000 capable of reaching the USSR. As if this was not enough, the superpowers also invested heavily in maintaining military bases overseas. The Americans had over 300. With the help of their allies in NATO and the Warsaw Pact, the superpowers could get troops to the 'front line' between capitalism and communism (wherever that happened to be) in only a few hours. By the early 1980s, as you can see from Source 6, the whole world was the superpowers' potential battleground.

Since superpower bases provided welcome employment opportunities in many poorer parts of the world, they were often welcomed by local communities – even though they knew that 'their' base might, one day, become a prime target for a deadly nuclear attack.

Afghanistan

Ordinary people could become caught up in superpower conflicts in other ways, too. Until 1979, the superpower forces, operating throughout the world, seemed locked in a dangerous, but fairly stable, 'balance of terror'. But then the Soviet Union invaded Afghanistan to try and restore to power the pro-communist government it had been backing. A long, bloody and INCONCLUSIVE civil war followed between Soviet troops (there were over 100,000 in Afghanistan by 1983) and the 'mujaheddin' – guerrilla fighters who received massive support from the USA. Cities were bombed and many parts of the countryside were made almost uninhabitable by landmines. Between 3 and 5 million civilians (one-third of the population) fled as refugees.

SOURCE 8

In the late fifties and early sixties when the West was pouring money into India's rural electrification programme, the [USSR's] People's Publishing House was distributing free copies of the Koran and the Mahabharata printed in Moscow. But only to those households which had been connected. The people enjoying the blessings of this new luxury, electricity, which illuminated their holy books in the dark, invariably said 'these Russians are great people.'

(Quote by a modern historian, J. Garrison, 1983.)

SOURCE 9

US forces must be capable of dealing with Soviet aggression in any area – Europe, the Persian Gulf, Northeast Asia, or elsewhere – both by defending in the given area and, if to our advantage, by exploiting Soviet VULNERABILITIES elsewhere at times and places of our choosing.

(From a secret memo from the US Defense Department (the Pentagon).)

QUESTIONS

1 *Does the growing stockpile of weapons mean that the SALT agreement were pointless?*

2 *Explain why Afghanistan has been described as 'Russia's Vietnam'?*

Was the Cold War worthwhile?

For both superpowers, the cost of constantly manufacturing new missile systems, and of taking part in numerous 'minor' wars during the 1970s and early 1980s, was very high. Ten per cent of the American government's budget, and around 20 per cent of the USSR's, was devoted to military spending. Often, to the protestors' anger, there did not seem to be enough left over to meet peaceful social needs (Source 10).

Economic warfare

Among the superpowers, economic problems were worse in the USSR (Source 11), though there was poverty in America, too. In spite of Khrushchev's economic and agricultural reforms, basic foodstuffs were still sometimes in short supply. They then had to be imported, and the Soviet government often found it hard to afford the high prices charged in the world-wide market place. Its economy was weak, its technology old-fashioned. Output was low, and goods were shoddy, compared with items made in the West. Few nations wanted to buy industrial or consumer goods made in the USSR, so the government earned very little foreign currency through its export trade.

The USA was (and still is) the world's largest exporter of grain. It needed to sell, and so, in spite of its political rivalry with the USSR, it was quite happy to trade with the Soviet government in grain and other basic foods. It even sent grain on credit (buy now, pay later) or SUBSIDISED (in effect reduced) the price of its exports, when Soviet stocks of foreign currency were running low. In economic terms, this was genuinely helpful; but there was a political price to pay. Source 12 explains what that was. The USSR was being squeezed.

Damage to the environment

All through the 1950s and 1960s – and into the 1980s, as well – the superpowers used remote areas of the world to test nuclear weapons. The USA used desert areas in the south-west US and islands in the Pacific. The USSR used the remote steppes of Central Asia for its nuclear explosions. Tests are now carried out underground, but at

SOURCE 10

We are allowing all this (the arms race) to happen while at the same time (1983) there are around the world:

870,000,000 adults who cannot read and write

500,000,000 people who have no jobs or are less than fully employed

130,000,000 children who are unable to attend primary school

450,000,000 people who suffer from hunger or MALNUTRITION

12,000,000 babies who die every year before their first birthday

42,000,000 people who are blind or nearly so

2,000,000,000 people who do not have safe water to drink

250,000,000 people who live in urban slums or shanty towns

(British anti-nuclear campaigners' leaflet, 1983.)

▲ **SOURCE 11**
Drabness and poverty in the USSR in the 1970s.

that time they were carried out in the open. The nuclear fallout (deadly cancer-causing pollution) from these explosions caused damage to the environment, to people living nearby, or those who took part in the testing. Today people seriously injured by atomic fallout are fighting for COMPENSATION and free medical care (Source 13).

There was another, equally dangerous, nuclear threat. Although it was strenuously denied by superpower governments at the time, some nuclear power station complexes played an important part in processing dangerous RADIOACTIVE by-products from nuclear weapons manufacture. They were an essential part of the nuclear weapons programme and a major pollution threat. Furthermore, as the escape of deadly radioactive particles from Three Mile Island power station (in Pennsylvania, USA, 1979) and, later, Chernobyl (in the Ukraine, then part of the USSR, 1986) showed, they could be very dangerous (Source 14). They could be very expensive, too. The clean-up operation after the relatively minor leak at Three Mile Island cost $1,000 million.

SOURCE 15

We [the US Government] should not provide the trade and credits necessary to prop up the Soviet economy except in exchange for specific and meaningful Soviet actions that promote stability, peace, and the well-being of everyone, including the citizens of the Soviet Union.

(Speech by senior US Presidential Adviser, Thomas C. Reed, 1982.)

◀ **SOURCE 13** Local Kazakh villagers protesting at the Soviet nuclear test site at Semipalatinsk in Central Asia, 1990.

▼ **SOURCE 14** An aerial view of the Chernobyl nuclear power plant after the explosion and fire in 1986.

*Q*UESTIONS

1 *Why was the Cold War so expensive?*

2 *How did the people of the USA and USSR feel this expense?*

3 *Which was more able to bear the expense of the Cold War: the USA or USSR? Explain your answer.*

4 *Find out about the links between the nuclear power and the nuclear weapons programmes.*

5 *How have they both caused danger even though nuclear weapons have never been used in war since 1945?*

Collective protests, individual freedom

Increasingly, protesters and peace campaigners during the 1970s and early 1980s in the USA and the USSR began to question not only the costs and risks involved in nuclear weapons, but the whole basis of the Cold War. The USA and the USSR both claimed to be struggling to bring about a 'good' society for their citizens. But at what cost? Could any government that killed so many people and spent so much on weapons of destruction really be called 'good'?

Source 15 expresses this attitude very well. What use is ideology – American or Soviet – when we are all dead? Surely individual lives and our common humanity are much more important than rival political views?

Babies not bombs

The women who protested against the arrival of Cruise missiles at the American air force base of Greenham Common (in southern England) in 1983, took this humane protest one step further (Source 16). They did not glory in NATO's military strength, or feel reassured by the strong American 'protective arm'. They refused to admire the very advanced technology of the Cruise missiles themselves. Instead, they chose to make their protest against nuclear weapons by pinning babies' clothes on to the air-base's barbed wire fence.

By deliberately contrasting the weakness and vulnerability of small children – the future of our planet – with the deadly Cruise missiles, the women protesters made a powerful moral statement: babies not bombs.

The Greenham Common protesters – and others, like them, who demonstrated at American nuclear bases throughout Europe – faced considerable opposition. People called them unpatriotic, or communist sympathisers, or politically stupid, or weak, or naive. Some protesters may have been all – or any – of these, but most were simply calling for a change of heart on the part of NATO governments, and for a society based not on hatred and aggression against an 'evil' Cold War enemy, but on kinder, gentler ideals.

SOURCE 15

Not even the most passionate IDEOLOGUE will be able to tell the ashes of capitalism from those of communism, for, among other reasons, he too will be dead.

(Comment by the American liberal economist, J. K. Galbraith, 1982)

▲ **SOURCE 16**
The Greenham Common protest.

SOURCE 17

Servile psychiatrists . . . describe concern for social problems as 'mental illness', can declare a man insane for being too passionate or for being too calm, for the brightness of his talents or for his lack of them. . . .

It is time to understand that the imprisonment of sane persons in madhouses because they have minds of their own is spiritual murder, a variation on gas chambers and even more cruel; the condemned suffer torments more fruitful and more prolonged. Like the gas chambers, those crimes will never be forgotten, and those involved will be condemned for all time, during their life and after death.

(Solzhenytsin, protesting at the imprisonment of Soviet scientist and protester Zhores Medvedev by the USSR government in 1970.)

QUESTIONS

1 *What differences were there between anti-Cold War protests in the West and in the USSR?*

2 *What similarities were there?*

The Greenham Common women did not win. The Cruise missiles stayed in Europe until they were withdrawn by the American government in 1989.

Soviet protests

There were protests against nuclear weapons in the Soviet Union, too. Distinguished scientists, like Andrei Sakharov and his wife, Yelena Bonner, campaigned with great courage against nuclear weapons and polluting nuclear tests. After accepting the Nobel Peace Prize for his writing and campaigning, Sakharov was harassed and persecuted by the Soviet government. He was exiled to the sinister 'closed' town of Gorky in 1980 and only released in 1986, after pressure from the international scientific community and a radical change in the Soviet government. (You can read more about this on pages 52 to 57.) Even then, he did not give up. He continued anti-nuclear campaigning until his death, aged 68, in 1989.

Because of his well-known scientific career, Sakharov's case received publicity outside the USSR. Source 17, written by another famous Soviet dissident, Aleksandr Solzhenitsyn, describes how thousands of other brave, mostly unknown, individuals dared to speak out against the Soviet authorities, and how they were treated. Like the Western protesters against nuclear weapons, they all wanted government attitudes and policies to change. Like the Greenham women, they were making a moral point. They felt that fear, torture and repression were too high a price to pay for 'strong' Soviet rulers, dedicated to keeping tight control of the communist world, and opposing the USA.

FOCUS ...*Solidarity*

While protesters like Sakharov were being imprisoned in the USSR, there were new protests in other communist states. In 1970, 20 Polish protesters were shot in the streets for arranging a demonstration; in 1976, electrician Lech Walesa (right) lost his job for daring to draw up a list of workers' grievances, then showing them to the management of the huge shipyards at Gdansk.

In 1980, Walesa climbed back into the Gdansk shipyards, and spoke to a meeting of 17,000 workers, urging them to strike and to campaign for freedom and justice. Together, they could achieve something tremendous, he believed. They agreed to his proposal, and the trade union 'Solidarity' was born. Strikers then demanded the right for their union to be free and independent of the Communist Party – and brought the whole of the northern coast of Poland to a standstill, until the government agreed to their demands.

Members of Solidarity were motivated by a variety of different views – some were socially conservative and Roman Catholic; others were radical, and wanted social and political reforms, as

well as freedom from Brezhnev-style Soviet control. They were all very anti-communist.

Solidarity grew rapidly, and members soon began to demand greater political freedom for all workers in Poland, as well as economic re-organisation. In 1981, there was an economic crisis in Poland, made worse by bad harvests. A state of emergency was declared, and a new, hard-line communist Prime Minister, General Jaruzelski, was appointed. He imprisoned many of the Solidarity leaders, including Walesa, and outlawed the entire movement in 1982. Lech Walesa was awarded the Nobel Peace Prize in 1983.

Solidarity continued to exist, underground, until 1989, when it was made legal once more. The communists were defeated in elections and Walesa was elected President of Poland in 1990.

The end of the

In December 1989, the two most powerful men in the world met on board a storm-tossed warship. The purpose of their meeting was truly historic. They had met to agree to end the Cold War.

In this Unit, we will look at the astonishing political changes that took place in the USSR and Eastern Europe between 1985 and 1991. We shall see how they affected relations between the two superpowers – and shaped the future of the world.

▲ SOURCE 1
Mikhail Gorbachev, soon after he came to power, meeting Russian people informally – something unheard of from previous Soviet leaders.

Key Questions

Why did the Cold War come to an end?

What changes in the USA and the USSR made this possible?

Are the Cold War superpowers still as powerful?

Has the end of the Cold War led to a 'new world order'?

In 1985, Soviet leader Konstantin Chernenko died. During his time in office, Cold War tensions between the USA and the USSR had increased, largely because of US President Reagan's 'Star Wars' plans (see page 44).

Mikhail Gorbachev (Source 1), the man who replaced Chernenko as Soviet leader, was a very different character, and had very different ideas. Although Gorbachev was only in power for five and a half years (1985–1991), under his rule the USSR was transformed. For the first time since the Russian Revolution of 1917, state controls on the economy and society were lifted, and the Communist Party lost its MONOPOLY position in political life. Western capitalist companies were even allowed to open branches in the heart of Moscow (Source 2).

You can read more about Gorbachev and his policies on pages 54 to 57. But first we should think about two questions. Why did Gorbachev start changing the Soviet Union? And what effect did the changes he introduced have on the Cold War?

Ripe for change

In 1986, in Moscow, Mikhail Gorbachev declared that 'Soviet society is ripe for change'. During the Brezhnev years, pressure for reform had been building up. The Soviet people

Cold War

SOURCE 2
Western business, and tastes, in a Russian city.

SOURCE 3 ►
Soviet engineers preparing to destroy missiles under the terms of the INF Treaty.

The result was corruption, absenteeism, alcoholism, drug abuse and increasing crime. Criticism of the Communist Party, government leaders and local conditions circulated in 'samizdat' (underground) newspapers, novels and poems. People felt bitter, cynical and, sometimes, depressed.

There were economic problems, too. Gorbachev realised that Soviet trade and industry urgently needed reform. The economy was becoming STAGNANT: output was falling, the quality of goods was poor, and costs were high. Farming and manufacturing both depended on large government subsidies. Even worse, arms spending was swallowing up almost 25% of the country's wealth, leaving less for other services, such as healthcare.

The beginning of the end?
In 1986, Gorbachev made a keynote speech to the Communist Party Congress, announcing dramatic changes to Soviet foreign policy, as well as plans for reforms at home. The USSR would work to eliminate all the nuclear weapons in the world by AD 2000. In return, Gorbachev demanded that America halt its 'Star Wars' weapons scheme.

To many members of government, in Moscow and Washington, this seemed like an impossible dream. But, within 18 months, Gorbachev and Reagan had signed an INF (Intermediate Nuclear Forces) treaty, agreeing to eliminate Soviet and American intermediate-range nuclear warheads, and to halt work on 'Star Wars' weapons. There were doubts on both sides over verification (making sure that weapons really were being disarmed). Nevertheless, the INF Treaty was formally ratified by June 1988. Was this the beginning of the end of the Cold War?

and their lifestyles had changed, but the Communist Party and the USSR government had not. Soviet society was no longer made up of illiterate peasants living on remote country farms, as it had been at the time of the Russian Revolution in 1917. Now, over 60% of the population lived in towns, and over 70% had

received a senior school education. News about the outside world reached the Soviet people via 87 million television sets and 83 million radios, even though it was often censored. Many people were eager for change, but, because of strict Communist Party control, they felt powerless to achieve it.

'Jaw, jaw not war, war'

How did the USA respond to changes in the USSR?

President Reagan of the USA was first elected in 1980, on a strongly anti-communist manifesto. He was re-elected in 1984, with a large majority, after campaigning even more vigorously against the USSR. We saw, on page 43, how he described the Soviet Union as an 'evil empire'. Yet this was not the whole picture. At one level, Reagan felt it was his duty to parade the USA's strength as 'leader of the free world', and not appear weak in the face of Soviet power. It certainly helped him win elections. At another level, even before Gorbachev came to power, he was interested in ending the Cold War. Even in the USA, the richest country in the world, some politicians and many members of the public were concerned about the amount of money being spent on weapons. President Reagan himself was worried about the possibility of nuclear war.

Previous Soviet leaders had felt the same about military spending and appearing resolutely opposed to the USA. Both superpowers seemed locked into an endless Cold War. But now, in 1985 and 1986, Gorbachev was not behaving like previous Soviet leaders. He seemed to be offering friendship, co-operation, nuclear disarmament, and peace.

American government representatives (Vice-President Bush and Secretary of State Schultz) first met Gorbachev at Chernenko's funeral in Moscow. On their return to the USA, Bush and Schultz presented very favourable reports of the new Soviet leader to President Reagan. Gorbachev was young (54), energetic, highly intelligent and had a warm sense of humour. He was brisk, clearheaded and could make quick decisions. Reagan and his advisers decided that here was someone they could negotiate with. It might not be easy, but it was worth a try. Now, for the first time in many years, both superpowers seemed to be aiming at the same goal. Reagan was reported to have joked using Churchill's phrase that 'Jaw, jaw [that is, lots of talking] is better than war, war.'

▲ SOURCE 4
Reagan and Gorbachev at talks in Iceland, 1986.

▼ SOURCE 5
The break-up of the Soviet 'empire'.

The 'talking' (long meetings between American and Soviet diplomats) went on for over a year before Reagan and Gorbachev first met, in Reykjavik, in Iceland, in 1986 (Source 4). It was not an easy meeting, but it was a beginning, and future meetings were soon arranged. These went well. When Gorbachev visited Washington in 1987, he was greeted by friendly crowds chanting 'Gorby, Gorby'. Far more important, he and Reagan signed the historic INF Treaty, banning all medium-range nuclear missiles. The next year (1988) Reagan visited Moscow, and this meeting was another diplomatic success. There was still a little mistrust, however, at least on the American side.

Gorbachev and Eastern Europe

Gorbachev was sympathetic to Eastern European demands for freedom. He had no wish to repeat the tragic Soviet invasions of Hungary (1956) and Czechoslovakia (1968). But at times, the pace of change seemed to be dizzyingly, dangerously fast. And many Communist leaders at home in the USSR felt that Gorbachev was 'giving away' countries that rightfully belonged – as allies – to the Soviet superpower bloc.

The political map of Europe was changing overnight, as the map in Source 5 and the time line opposite shows). Moreover, the enlarged European Community was playing an increasingly important economic and political role. The new, free nations of Eastern Europe now hoped for friendship and help from Brussels, rather than from the USSR.

Assessment

1 *Gorbachev was taking an immense gamble by offering to end the Cold War. How did he think an end to the Cold War would benefit the USSR?*

2 *Do you think his gamble worked?*

3 *Did Gorbachev end the Cold War single-handed?*

Time chart

Events 1985–1991

1980 Ronald Reagan elected President of USA.
1984 Ronald Reagan elected for a second 4-year term as President.
1985 Soviet leader Konstantin Chernenko dies. Mikhail Gorbachev becomes leader of USSR. Introduces policies of 'glasnost' (openness) and 'perestroika' (restructuring the economy).
1985 Reagan and Gorbachev meet in Geneva.
1986 Andrei Sakharov (see page 51) and others released from exile.
1986 Reagan and Gorbachev meet in Iceland.
1987 Reagan and Gorbachev meet in Washington. USA and USSR agree INF (Intermediate-range Nuclear Forces) Treaty.
1988 President Reagan visits Moscow for meeting with Gorbachev; INF Treaty ratified (confirmed).
1989 George Bush becomes President of the USA after winning elections in 1988.
1989 Solidarity Trade Union legalised in Poland (see page 51).
1989 Anti-communist demonstrations in Czechoslovakia.
1989 Anti-communist demonstrations in Bulgaria.
1989 Gorbachev sets up Congress of People's Deputies in Moscow – free discussion of government policies now allowed.
1989 Gorbachev visits China. First USSR–China summit since 1959.
1989 Opening of Berlin Wall.
1989 Bush and Gorbachev meet in Malta, to declare the Cold War officially over.
1989 Communist leader Ceausescu shot dead in Romania; mass pro-democracy protests.
1990 East and West Germany re-unified.
1990 United Germany becomes a member of NATO, with Gorbachev's agreement.
1990 Albania (formerly isolated, extreme communist) announces plans to establish diplomatic relations with the USA, as well as with USSR (its former ally, before a major quarrel in 1958). There are pro-democracy rallies and government reforms.
1990 Free elections in Bulgaria; Socialists (formerly Communists) narrowly win, but are soon replaced.
1990 Free elections in Hungary; Communists lose control.
1990 Civil war threatens in Yugoslavia as ancient ethnic and religious rivalries become entangled with demands for political freedom from collapsing communist rule.
1990 START (Strategic Arms Reduction Treaty) agreed between USA and USSR.
1990 New political parties allowed to be formed in USSR. Communist Party no longer has monopoly.
1990 Anti-communist Lech Walesa (see page 51) wins free elections in Poland.
1990 Breakaway movements in Baltic States: Lithuania and Latvia declare independence from USSR. Estonia begins negotiations for independence.
1990 Free elections in Czechoslovakia; Communists lose control. Czechoslovakia leaves Comecon (USSR-led Communist economic alliance); divides into Czech and Slovak Republics.
1990 Boris Yeltsin becomes President of Russian Soviet Socialist Republic (one of the member states of USSR).
1991 Political tensions in USSR; quarrels between old-style Communists and reformers, inspired by Gorbachev's ideas. Yeltsin backs reformers, who win.
1991 USSR breaks up into many separate independent states, in spite of Gorbachev's efforts to maintain unity.
1991 Gorbachev resigns.
1991 Yeltsin becomes President of new independent state of Russia.

The Cold War ends

Why did the USA and the USSR decide to end the Cold War?

The winter of 1989–1990 was an exciting time. In November 1989, the crossing points in the Berlin Wall (for so long one of the most hated symbols of the Cold War) were opened, and the Wall itself began to be torn down (Source 6). Citizens of East and West Germany, separated by armed force since 1945, hugged one another and danced for joy in the streets. Early in 1990, free elections were held all over Eastern Europe (see Source 5 on page 54), and even in the USSR. Almost everywhere, the old communist regimes were toppled from power (Source 7).

President Bush of the USA was not a man who normally welcomed excitements and upheavals. Yet Gorbachev's willingness to let Eastern European states decide their own future convinced him that the time was right for the USA to join with the USSR and declare that the Cold War was at an end. Like the Soviet Union, the USA wanted peace. But both governments had another motive, too. They wanted to work together to maintain a degree of stability in international affairs. Too much change, too fast, might be dangerous. The American and Soviet leaders met to declare the Cold War officially over in December 1989. This historic moment was celebrated in President Bush's optimistic speech (Source 8).

Inside the USSR

The USA and USSR were now friends, the Cold War nuclear threat had retreated, and people in many parts of the world breathed a sigh of relief. But Mikhail Gorbachev still faced serious problems. There were demands for freedom from many member states of the USSR, especially the Baltic republics (Lithuania, Latvia and Estonia), which had been seized by Stalin during the Second World War. Here, Gorbachev surprised some people. In contrast to his attitude towards Eastern Europe, he refused to grant the Baltic states their independence, because he believed it would lead to the break-up of the USSR. Even so, two Baltic countries (Latvia and Lithuania) declared themselves independent in 1990.

▲ **SOURCE 6**
The Berlin Wall coming down, November 1989.

▼ **SOURCE 7**
Thousands of demonstrators pack the main square in Prague as the Czech communist regime collapses.

SOURCE 8

Not so long ago, some believed that the weight of history condemned our two great countries, our two great peoples, to permanent confrontation. Well, you and I must challenge history, make new strides, build a relationship of enduring co-operation.

We may not agree on everything, and indeed we don't agree on everything, but we believe in one great truth: the world has waited long enough; the Cold War must end.

(President Bush declares the Cold War 'over', December 1989.)

Soon afterwards, the important state of Russia elected as its leader Boris Yeltsin, Gorbachev's great rival, who held even more reformist views. Many of those who supported Gorbachev's ideas felt that more rapid change was needed. On the other hand, many old-style communists resented the changes. The demands from some pats of the USSR for greater freedom from central control increased. It seemed as if the USSR was beginning to break up whether Gorbachev approved or not.

Even in Moscow, the USSR's capital city, many Soviet citizens were reluctant to follow Gorbachev's policies of glasnost and perestroika (see fact box opposite). Many Soviet people did not feel ready for such drastic change. Living standards declined, and organised crime increased.

Worse was to come. Old-style Soviet politicians and generals accused Gorbachev of wrecking their 'motherland'. They protested against his policies, and in August 1991 tried to take over the country. Gorbachev was put under house arrest. Yeltsin defied the rebels and rallied support. The rebellion failed and Gorbachev briefly returned to power. But things had changed: the member states of the USSR declared themselves indepedent and by the end of the year the Soviet Union ceased to exist. Gorbachev was forced to resign.

Glasnost and perestroika

Gorbachev wanted to revive the USSR's stagnant economy by improving output, markets and technology. This programme he called **perestroika** (restructuring). However, he also realised that it would only work if people were given more freedom and a greater say in how the country was run. He therefore also pursued **glasnost** (openness), which allowed freedom of debate, media freedom and more freedom from government control.

'We have abandoned the claim to have a monopoly on the truth; we no longer think that we are the best and that we are always right, that those who disagree with us are our enemies. We have now decided . . . to base our policy on the principle of freedom of choice, . . . and to develop our culture through dialogue . . . Briefly, this is the essence of perestroika's philosophy; we are getting to know ourselves, revealing ourselves to the world, and discovering the world.'

Gorbachev speaking in Rome in 1987 about his policy of perestroika.

Assessment

1 Gorbachev's career has been summarised as follows by one historian:

'Hailed as a hero in the West, at home he was regarded with some hostility by both conservatives within the Communist Party and by reformers who considered the pace of liberalisation too slow.'

Can you explain why opinions about Gorbachev varied so widely?

2 *Do you think Gorbachev was a hero or a failure? Explain why.*

F●CUS ...*Mikhail Gorbachev*

Mikhail Gorbachev was born in 1931 to a peasant family living in Stavropol in the Caucasus. From 1946, he worked as a machine operator. In 1952, he joined the Communist Party. In 1953, he went to Moscow University, where he studied law. After leaving university, Gorbachev returned to Stavropol, where he was put in charge of local collective farms. He also ran the local Komsomol (Young Communist League). In 1970, he became Secretary of the regional Communist Party.

In 1978, Gorbachev moved to Moscow, to become an official of the central committee of the Soviet Communist Party, with special responsibility for farming. In 1980, he became a member of the Politburo (the all-powerful ruling body of the USSR Communist Party).

In 1985, Gorbachev became General Secretary of the Soviet Communist Party – that is, leader of the government of the USSR. Together with his wife Raisa he embarked on policies of glasnost (openness) and perestroika (restructuring) – see fact box.

Raisa Gorbacheva was a professional sociologist, and the first Soviet leader's wife to play an important public role. She was described by one British historian as 'a woman of considerable intelligence and obvious charm . . . in an unsettled [Soviet] society, she attracted criticism, but abroad she added to her husband's political and popular prestige and did a great deal to make a success of East–West arms talks'.

A peace dividend?

▲ SOURCE 9
Fighting in the former Yugoslavia,
1993. A destroyed Bosnian village.

▲ SOURCE 10
Haitian refugees being picked up by
US coastguards from their small boat.

Sadly, the end of the Cold War did not lead to lasting world peace. Far from it. In fact, two of the most miserable scenarios unfolded in former superpower 'client' states, Yugoslavia and Haiti.

Yugoslavia

Since 1945, Yugoslavia had been ruled by Josip Tito (1892–1980), a communist of a strongly individual kind. Yugoslavia was composed of many different ethnic and religious groups; the land had been fought over for centuries, and was traditionally home to many rival warlords and mountain bandit bands. During Tito's lifetime, Yugoslavia remained unified, partly because of the force of his personality, and partly because of the respect he had won for his patriotic fight against Nazi invaders during the Second World War.

After Tito's death, the collective leadership he had appointed to continue ruling soon quarrelled among themselves, and, by 1990, separatist, anti-communist governments had set themselves up in four of Yugoslavia's regions. Bitter fighting broke out in 1991, and included horrific episodes of 'ETHNIC CLEANSING' and long-drawn-out

sieges (Source 9). United Nations intervention failed to stop the fighting. An uneasy peace was finally arranged at the end of 1995.

Haiti

The Caribbean nation of Haiti had been supported by the USA for many years, to protect its commercial interests and to try and halt communist influence. In 1957, Dr François Duvalier (known as 'Papa Doc') was elected president. He was followed by his son Jean-Claude ('Baby Doc'), who ruled from 1971 to 1986. Both relied on a fearsome secret police force to stay in power.

Anti-government riots began in 1984, and in 1986 the Americans helped Baby Doc escape. They set up a new Haitian 'puppet' government in 1987, but violence and economic crisis followed. Boatloads of refugees desperately tried to make the illegal and dangerous sea-crossing to the Florida coast of the USA. Thousands drowned, and most who reached the USA were INTERNED in camps then sent back home (Source 10).

In 1990, a new popular president, Jean-Baptiste Aristide, a former priest, was

Assessment

1 The Cold War lasted 45 years. Who, if anyone, benefited from it?

2 Who suffered from it?

3 Who has benefited from the end of the Cold War?

4 Did the USA 'win' the Cold War? Did the USSR 'lose'?

5 One of the main causes of the Cold War was misunderstanding. Do US and Russian leaders understand each other better no than Truman and Stalin did (see Unit 1)?

elected. Though democratic, high-principled and well-meaning, he was unable to solve many of Haiti's problems. Most people were extremely poor; there was economic stagnation, high unemployment, rising crime, malnutrition, disease, a drug problem and, increasingly, the spread of AIDS.

Aristide was then overthrown by the Haitian army, which ruled for two years in the face of international disapproval, before the USA intervened to restore Aristide in 1994. In the meantime, the plight of Haiti's poorest had only become worse.

Rich world, poor world

As well as failing to solve crises in individual superpower client states, the ending of the Cold War failed to solve a much larger crisis facing the whole world – the gap between rich and poor nations. Large sums of money were no longer being spent on Cold War weapons – but they were not re-directe1d to help fight world poverty, either. Wars continued in places such as Somalia and Rwanda separate from superpower rivalry.

Uncertain futures

Instead, in the early 1990s, both superpowers found themselves increasingly preoccupied by money worries and quarrels over policy at home. In the USA, there was unemployment, poverty and racial tensions. There were fierce debates between 'right-wing' Republicans and liberal Democrats over how much money the government should spend on welfare and the role of government in people's lives.

In the USSR, there was corruption, organised crime, insecurity, poverty and food shortages. The old central government 'safety-net', which kept the whole population housed and fed, could no longer be relied upon to work. Some politicians wanted to go back to the 'good old days' of Communist Party rule; others advocated an aggressively capitalist economy, or called for a new spirit of nationalism, based on pride in Russia's ancient traditions and military power.

Political and economic instability in many former Soviet lands with non-Russian populations (see Source 11 for an example) have led to continued fighting and terrible suffering.

Aeronautical
To do with the building of aircraft.

Allies
Allies are people or countries that agree to help and support each other, usually against a common threat.

Amalgamate
When organizations areamalgamed, they join together.

Annihilation
Total destruction.

Atheistic
Not believing in God or any organised religion.

Atomic bomb
A nuclear bomb which uses the splitting of atoms to create a huge explosion.

Bloc
A group of countries with a common interest or aim.

Bourgeois
Belonging to the middle class.

Capitalism
An economic and political system where property and business are owned by individuals, not by the state, and in which there is competition to creat profits.

Censor
Examine writing or film before it is published or shown in order to cut out parts which are thought unacceptable.

Cold War
State of hostility betweencountries, stopping short of actual warfare. Usually used to refer to the conflict between the West (led by the USA) and the communist countries (led by the USSR).

Colonialism
A system in which one country conquers and controls other territories and uses their resources to increase its own power and wealth.

Communism
A system of government in which the state is in charge of producing everything, and in which there is no private property.

Compensation
Money given to make up for loss or something bad that has happened to a person.

Containment
Keeping a country's power within limits and not letting it spread any further.

Democracy
A system of government in which leaders are chosen by the people by voting.

Détente
A friendly relationship between countries instead of mistrust (from French word meaning relaxation).

Dictatorship
A system of government where one person has complete control.

Disarmament
The process of reducing some or all of a country's store of weapons.

Ethnic cleansing
A word used to describe the killing or brutal driving out of members of other races from a mixed area so as to leave one ethnic group in complete control.

Guerrilla
Part of an unofficial army. usually fighting against a stronger organised army by means of surprise tactics.

Ideologue
Someone who believes in an *ideology* and who tries to put it into action.

Ideology
A set of political beliefs.

Imperialism
A political system in which a rich and powerful country controls other countries.

Inconclusive
Without a clear result.

Internment
Being interned is being put into prison, usually because you are from another country and have entered illegally and will not be allowed to stay permanently.

Iron Curtain
The border between the USSR and its allies and Western Europe. Described as an 'iron curtain' by Churchill in his speech at Fulton, USA, in 1946.

Malnutrition
Made weak because of lack of food.

Media
Newspapers, radio and television.

Monopoly
Sole control.

Nationalise
Taken out of private hands and put under the control of the state.

Nationalist
Support of and belief in the importance of your own country.

Neutral
Not involved or not taking sides in a dispute.

Pessimistic
Believing the worst thing will happen.

Puppet government
A government controlled like a puppet by a more powerful one.

Radioactive
A substance which gives off harmful energy in the form of invisible but dangerous rays.

Satellite
Man-made object sent into space to send back information or be part of a communications network. The word can also be used to describe those countries which a more powerful country controls.

Silo
Store.

Stagnant
Little or no economic growth.

Subjugation
The complete control of a group of people, usually by force.

Subsidise
A subsidy is money paid by a government to make a product cheaper for people to buy.

Superpower
A very powerful country, usually with nuclear weapons.

Vulnerable
Weak and open to attack.

INDEX

Page numbers in **bold** refer to illustrations/captions.

List of abbreviations

Comecon	Council for Mutual Economic Aid
Cominform	Communist Information Bureau
Comintern	Communist International
DDR	German Democratic Republic (East Germany)
FDR	Federal Republic of Germany (West Germany)
ICBM	Intercontinental Ballistic Missile
INF	Intermediate Nuclear Forces
MIRV	Multiple Independently targeted Re-entry Vehicle
NATO	North Atlantic Treaty Organisation
OEEC	Organisation for European Economic Development
SALT	Strategic Arms Limitation Treaty
SEATO	South East Asia Treaty Organisation
START	Strategic Arms Reduction Talks
UNO	United Nations Organisation
USA	United States of America
USSR	Union of Socialist Soviet Republics

ACKNOWLEDGEMENTS

Every effort has been made to contact the holders of copyright material but if any have been inadvertently overlooked, the publishers will be pleased to make the necessary arrangements at the first opportunity.

The publishers would like to thank the following for permission to reproduce photographs on these pages:

T = top, B = bottom, C = centre, L = left

Cartoon by Illingworth, *Daily Mail*, Centre for Study of Cartoons and Caricature, University of Kent, Canterbury/Solo Syndication 36T; Cartoon by Jim Borgman, reproduced by kind permission of King Features Synidicate Inc. 17; Corbis-Bettman 4, 6L, 28T, 44T, 57; Corbis-Bettman/Reuter 3T, 56T; Corbis-Bettman/UPI 3B, 22, 28B, 29, 32B, 35R, 36B, 42–43, 47, 48; ET Archive 23L; Hulton Getty King Collection 16–17, 18; United Artists/courtesy Kobal Collection 33B; Collections Musée Royal de l'Armée, Bruxelles 6R; Network: Michel Setboun/Rapho 23R, Paul Lowe 53T, John Sturrock 56B, Roger Hutchings 58L; Peter Newark's American Pictures 19; Novosti 49T, 52; Popperfoto 9, 20, 25R, 32T, 33T, 33C, 35L, 38T, 49B, 50, 51, 53B, 54, 59; Cartoons by E. H. Shepard 11, 14, *Punch*, reproduced by permission; Frank Spooner Pictures/Gamma 58R; © Ingram Pinn/The Sunday Times 24; Topham/AP 12,. 43; Topham Picturepoint 44B.

Cover photograph: Frank Spooner Pictures

The author and publishers gratefully acknowledge the following publications from which written sources in this book are drawn:

Daniel Snowman, *The USA: Twenties to Vietnam*, B. T. Batsford; J. Garrison and P. Shirpuri, *The Russian Threat – its myths and realities*, Gateway; D. Oberdorfer, *The Turn: How the Cold War Came to an End*, Jonathan Cape

Published in 1996 by Collins Educational
An imprint of HarperCollins*Publishers* Ltd
77–85 Fulham Palace Road
London W6 8JB

© HarperCollins*Publishers*

First published 1996
Reprinted 1997

ISBN 0 00 327009 2

Fiona Macdonald and Richard Staton assert the moral right to be identified as the authors of this work.

All rights reserved. No part of this publication may be reproduced, stored in a retrieval system, or transmitted in any form or by any means, electronic, mechanical, photocopying, recording or otherwise, without the prior permission of the publisher.

Edited by Lorimer Poultney
Book designed by Sally Boothroyd
Picture research by Celia Dearing
Production by Susan Cashin
Artwork by Julia Osorno

Printed and bound in Hong Kong

UNIVERSITY OF WOLVERHAMPTON
LEARNING RESOURCES